This book is just for

_____ and _____.

We're on our way towards building an even closer relationship.

Bonding While Learning

Bonding While Learning (First Edition, Revised)

Copyright © 2007 by America Learns, LLC. All rights reserved.

Published by America Learns, LLC
15455 San Fernando Mission Blvd.
Suite 309
Mission Hills, CA 91345

ISBN 978-0-6151-3829-9

Please submit changes or report errors to publishing@americalearns.net.

For information about special discounts for bulk purchases, please contact America Learns, LLC at 1-310-689-0542 or publishing@americalearns.net.

Published in the United States of America.

For more information, please visit http://americalearns.net.

Bonding While Learning

Activities to Grow Your Relationship
While Preparing for Reading Success

First Edition, Revised

Gary Lee Kosman & Grace May Chiu

Cover Illustration by Grace May Chiu
Inside Section Illustrations by Kim Carmel

Visit us on the Web at http://americalearns.net/families.

TABLE OF CONTENTS

ABOUT THIS BOOK

What *Bonding While Learning* is About

We created this book to help you spend meaningful, quality time with your child that not only builds your relationship but also supports your child's early literacy growth. While you'll always be able to purchase books of worksheets and electronic games for your child to practice specific skills, there won't always be time to develop those skills while forming closer bonds with one another. When you can create those bonds with smiles and hugs while preparing your child for reading success, what can be better?

Using the Book

Bonding While Learning is full of fun, engaging activities that you can use over several years. Many of the activities will provide you with answers to specific questions, while you can use others whenever you read or even take a walk with your child.

Since every child is unique and is ready to grasp new skills and knowledge at different stages, there's no need for you to go through the activities in the order they're listed. Use the activities to answer a specific question you have or when your child is ready for them. The top of each activity tells you when it's appropriate to use it.

So if your child is just beginning to recognize the letters of the alphabet, check out the activities in the section called "Recognizing the Letters of the Alphabet." If you're wondering how to help your child learn to write his or her name, check out the activity called Learning to Write and Recognize Your Name. If your child isn't ready to begin learning his or her letters, your child is never too young to be read to, so check out the sections called "Reading With Your Child" and "Understanding What You're Reading Together." Discover new parts of the book as your child continues to grow and learn with you.

The Materials You Need Are Already Here.

We want you and your child to spend as much time as possible doing these activities (rather than preparing for them), so we've included a wealth of the materials you'll need. Check out the materials section beginning on page 93.

Special Out-And-About Extension Activities™

Today's parents are often on the run with their children, taking them to the grocery store, to the doctor, to dinner with family and friends. Just because you're on the run doesn't mean you don't have time to grow closer with your child while supporting his or her learning. That's why many *Bonding While Learning* activities come with Out-And-About Extension Activities™ that you can use in the car, in line at the store, at a restaurant, and even in the pediatrician's waiting room.

Special At-Home Extension Activities

You can use *Bonding While Learning* activities almost anywhere, but some activities are especially good for home. Keep your eyes peeled for those activities with special At-Home Extension Activities for more ideas on spending quality bonding and learning time together.

THE BONDING WHILE LEARNING TEAM

Grace May Chiu, Co-Author & Cover Illustrator

Grace has worked with thousands of children and youth across the country as a National Blue Ribbon teacher, technology educator and literacy professional developer. She is not only a literacy expert in theory, but in practice as well, serving as America Learns' Reading Strategies Expert. She has also worked with young people in Los Angeles, Baltimore, and Boston. Grace is currently a Ph.D. candidate in Urban Education at the University of California.

Gary Lee Kosman, Co-Author

Gary is the founder and CEO of America Learns (www.americalearns.net), a premier national educational performance and accountability firm. The organization's flagship service, the America Learns Network, helps school districts, universities and community organizations track, evaluate and provide ongoing guidance and support to teachers, tutors and mentors. America Learns also creates and publishes high quality, meaningful, stress-free learning opportunities for children that are steeped in relevant research and practice. Gary has been involved in multiple facets of the education sector, from serving on the external evaluation team for the City of Los Angeles' LA's BEST after-school program to co-authoring *A Compact for Reading* (1999). He has also worked with The City of St. Louis' Head Start program, the Children's Math Worlds project, and the Los Angeles Times' Reading by 9 initiative. Gary spends much of his free time volunteering as a children's sports coach.

Kim Carmel, Inside Section Illustrator

Kim writes and does graphic design for several organizations, including the University of California, Spa magazine and others. In 2005, she co-created *Famous Pairs: A Deliciously Absurd Collection of Portraits*. When away from the computer, Kim enjoys running, photography and catching up on a good book.

ACKNOWLEDGEMENTS

We didn't do this alone. Our organization is built upon co-innovation, a process of getting input, feedback and support from as many intelligent, brutally honest people as possible in order to create and offer the most useful products and services for children.

Among the army of people who helped to bring *Bonding While Learning* to life, we'd especially like to thank:

• The thousands of teachers, tutors and mentors using the America Learns Network everyday who constantly share and inspire us with unique, engaging, thoughtful teaching practices, many of which you'll find adapted just for families in this book;

• Our summer 2006 summer interns, Matt Miller and Jennifer Chernick, both of whom put in countless hours on this project, with Matt doing much of the first round editing and Jennifer arranging and conducting interviews of parents nationwide to learn how we could make *Bonding While Learning* truly useful to young children and their families;

• Robyn Wasserman and Rachel Tronstein for spending countless hours reviewing and editing various drafts of this book;

• Gary's mother, stepmother, stepfather, and his Mimi, all of whom put in time and gave countless amounts of support to us as we went through the research, writing, editing and publishing processes; and to

• Echoing Green (www.echoinggreen.org), whose seed funding of our organization has allowed us to already reach more than 10,000 children in just a little over two years.

The One Activity That's Just for You:
Knowing When & How to Celebrate Your Child's Effort & Accomplishments

Why this page matters:

Children and adults need to practice what they're learning in order to master it. So if your child doesn't immediately grasp certain material in this book, know that that's okay and perfectly normal. The ideas on this page will help you celebrate your child's path towards mastering his or her new skills and knowledge.

The basics:

When celebrating your child's efforts or accomplishments, explicitly state what he or she did that led you to celebrate.

Example #1: Rather than saying, "Good Job," you can make specific statements such as:

"Nice job sounding out letter A!"

"I see you looking at the pictures to help you think about what will happen next. That's a great way to help you read! It shows me you're understanding what's going on with [character names]."

"You're asking such great questions about the story. Good for you!"

"You used to get so frustrated when you made a mistake that you stopped playing. Now, you don't let a little mistake upset or distract you. Instead, you stick with the activity and keep going! You should be proud of yourself; I am."

Example #2: Share how your child's efforts make you feel and ask your child how he or she feels.

"I love It when you _____."

"I'm proud that you worked so hard at _____."

"When you _____, I feel _____. How does it make you feel?"

Stay away from "take back praise."

For example, telling your child, "Nice job summarizing that story. **Why can't you do that every time?**" seems like praise, but comes across as a complaint about your child's regular practices. Children who hear praise like this may feel criticized, hurt or shamed.

Stay away from misleading praise.

If your child is having real problems with reading, it's misleading to say, "You're doing an excellent job" when both of you know that he or she isn't yet doing a wonderful job. You can still encourage your child by saying, "Here is one way I see you learning the letters of the alphabet: you know almost all of the letters and their sounds. You're doing a great job taking steps towards knowing all of the letters!"

What to do While Reading Together, page 3

Reading With Your Child

What to do While Reading Together

STEP 1:

Preview the book's illustrations with your child before reading.

Look at the cover and illustrations with your child before reading in order to get an idea of the book's contents and to get her thinking about what she already knows.

Here are some questions to ask: "Let's look at the cover. What do you see here? Based on the cover illustration, what do you think this book is going to be about? Now let's look through the pictures of the book. What do you think is happening in this picture? What do the pictures tell us about what may happen?"

STEP 2:

Before reading the book, ask your child to open it and find a common, simple word he already knows (such as a, at, is, to, me). You can write the word on a piece of paper.

Ask: "Are there any words you see that look familiar to you? Do you see the word **is** on this page?

Ask your child to locate an unknown word (not previously read in other texts), after you introduce, point, and pronounce the new word:

Say: "I'm going to show you a new word that's in this book. It's **the**. [Write the word **the**.] It's spelled t-h-e. [Point to each letter as you say the letter's name.] Can you find the word **the** on this page?"

(continued on following page)

STEP 3:

Model reading print from left to right and top to bottom. Also model how to point to each word accurately as it is read.

Say: "When we read, I want you to practice pointing to each word as we read it. Try to place your finger under the word, not on top of the word. If we put our fingers on top of the word, the word is hard to see."

STEP 4:

Prompt your child to make predictions while reading.

Before turning a page that may unfold an important part of the story, you may want to ask: "What do you think will happen next? Why do you think that?"

STEP 5:

Model and prompt self-monitoring (checking to see if you understand what's going on) and self-correcting (correcting your own reading errors).

Ask throughout your reading, particularly when your child scrunches up her face or looks bored or inattentive: "Is this making sense? What's happening to [name of character] here?"

STEP 6:

Help your child make relevant, personal connections to the book during and after reading.

Ask: "Does that picture (or sentence) remind you of something? What does it remind you of?"

Say: "Can you tell me what happened in the story? Show me your favorite part of the book. What do you like about it?"

If you've adopted a child whose primary language is not English and is just learning English: Keep in mind that your child's home language may be written in very different ways than the English language. For example, some languages are read from right to left, or from top to bottom where symbolic characters are read vertically. As you introduce the directionalilty of English print to your child, point out these differences, but avoid statements that place a right/wrong value on those differences. For example, you can say, "In English, we read from left to right," but do not say, "We read from left to right; reading from right to left is the WRONG way to read." Statements such as this can leave your child feeling that you are placing a negative value on his home language.

Keeping Your Child's Attention as You Read Aloud

WHEN TO USE THIS ACTIVITY:

Use this activity to help you keep your child focused while you read a story or other text aloud.

STEP 1:

Keep outside distractions to a minimum.

Try to find a quiet spot where you can read.

STEP 2:

Sit beside and close to your child (not across from him).

STEP 3:

Ask your child to select the book that you'll read aloud.

If you allow your child to select the book he wants you to read, you're more likely to have a captive audience. Before you begin reading, ask your child to share why he chose the book. Encourage him to make predictions about what's going to happen before you begin to read, as well as throughout the story.

STEP 4:

Ask your child to "fill in the words" as you read aloud.

If you're reading a highly patterned story (e.g., *I Know an Old Lady Who Swallowed a Fly* or *The Little Red Hen*) or one that contains repeated phrases (such as *Three Little Pigs*), see what happens when you pause after you say, "Then I'll huff, and I'll puff, and—". You'll find that your child enjoys filling in your words. He must pay attention in order to do it.

STEP 5:

Read with enthusiasm and expression!

Try to make the story come alive with different character voices and lots of expression. Notice what makes your child smile or laugh and keep doing it. Have fun!

Goldilocks and the Three Books
Selecting Books to Read with Your Child

WHEN TO USE THIS ACTIVITY:

You can help your child learn to begin picking out books for himself to read using the conversation points below. The conversations you'll have with your child will help him learn to tell the difference between *too easy*, *just right*, **and** *challenging books*.

MATERIALS

- A few books
- The "Goldilocks and the Three Bears" story on page 7
- Optional: Dolls or puppets to enhance your storytelling

STEP 1:

If your child isn't yet familiar with the story "Goldilocks and the Three Bears," read or tell him about the story. This story will serve as a foundation for your conversation around *too easy*, *just right*, and *too hard* books. You can find our version of the story on page 7.

STEP 2:

Next, tell your child a spin-off tale of "Goldilocks and the Three Books."

Your story might sound like this: "One day, Goldilocks entered the library because she was hungry for a good story. She picked up a chapter book and said, 'Oh my, this book is *too hard*,' and put it back.

Next, Goldilocks picked up a picture book entitled, 'My Baby's First Picture Book.' There weren't any words on the pages, just pictures of toys and fruit. 'Oh no, this book is *too easy*,' said the girl.

Finally, Goldilocks discovered a book where she knew most of the words and could understand the story from the words and the pictures. 'Alright, this book is *just right* for me!' She finished reading the book and put it back where she found it. The End!"

STEP 3:

Talk with your child about how to pick *just right* books when he reads.

Discuss: "You can be like Goldilocks and choose the just right book. What happens when we pick a book that is too hard? What happens when we pick a book that is too easy? I want you to become a great reader and the best way to do that is to find books where we know most of the words, learn some new words, and understand what's going on."

GOLDILOCKS AND THE THREE BEARS

Once upon a time there was a little girl named Goldilocks who lived at the edge of a great forest. She was called Goldilocks because she had beautiful, curly blond hair that gleamed like gold.

Goldilocks could sometimes be naughty. Every day as Goldilocks went out to play, her mother would remind her: "Now Goldilocks, you may go and play in the meadow, but don't go into the forest or you will get lost."

One morning, Goldilocks began to get tired of playing in the meadow. "I know," said Goldilocks to herself, "I'll go exploring in the forest." She looked back at the house to make sure that her mother wasn't watching. Then she ran off across the meadow and into the forest.

Goldilocks wandered deeper and deeper into the forest. She wandered so far that she became completely lost. She felt very frightened and was about to cry when she saw a strange little cottage amongst the trees. Goldilocks tapped on the door -- tap, tap, tap -- but nobody answered. Then she peeped in through an open window. She didn't see anybody inside. Goldilocks decided to climb through the window into the cottage and look around.

Inside the cottage, a fire was burning brightly in the fireplace and a table was set for breakfast with three bowls of steaming oatmeal. It smelled delicious and Goldilocks realized how hungry she was. "I'll just try a little bit to see how it tastes," she said. First she tried the biggest bowl but the oatmeal was too hot. Then she tried the middle bowl but the oatmeal was too cold. Then she tried the little bowl and the oatmeal was just right. She ate it all up in just two minutes.

Goldilocks was tired and wanted to sit down. She noticed three chairs by the fireplace and walked over to them. First, she tried the biggest chair but it was way too high. Then, she tried the middle chair. That one was too high as well. She then tried the smallest chair, but it was too small. When she sat in the small chair to try it out, it broke to pieces and Goldilocks fell on the floor.

Goldilocks saw some stairs in a corner of the room and decided to climb to the top. She found a bedroom with three beds. One was very big, one was middle sized and one was very, very tiny. She tried the biggest bed, but it was just too hard. Then she tried the middle sized bed, but that was too soft. She then tried the smallest bed. That bed was just right. And after just one minute of lying on that bed, Goldilocks fell fast asleep.

Now, Goldilocks didn't know that the cottage belonged to three bears and that they were on their way home. Father Bear had been collecting wood for the fire. Mother Bear had collected a basket of blueberries. Baby Bear didn't do much today, but he was still very hungry when the family returned to their cottage. "I hope our oatmeal is cool enough to eat," said Baby Bear. "I'm so hungry.'"

When they came in they went straight to the table to eat their oatmeal. "Somebody has been eating my oatmeal," said Father Bear. "Somebody has been eating my oatmeal too," said Mother Bear. "Somebody ate all of my oatmeal," cried Baby Bear.

Then Father Bear noticed his chair. "Who has been sitting in my chair?" he roared. "Who has been sitting in my chair?" asked Mother Bear. "And who broke my chair to pieces?" cried Baby Bear.

The three Bears went upstairs. "Somebody has been lying on my bed," said Father Bear. "Somebody has been lying on my bed," said Mother Bear. "Somebody has been lying on my bed," cried Baby Bear, "and she's still there, fast asleep!"

The three Bears looked at the little girl. What was she doing in their cottage? Goldilocks woke up, looked at the bears, and become very frightened. "Oh no," she thought to herself. "The bears look so angry. I need to get out of here." She jumped out of bed, ran down the stairs and out the cottage door into the forest. She ran and ran, not stopping until she reached her own house with her mother waiting at the doorstep. She never went exploring in the forest again.

THE END

Quickly Reengaging Your Child in a Story You're Reading

WHEN TO USE THIS ACTIVITY:

Think about using this activity when your child begins to lose interest in a story you're reading together.

STEP 1:

When your child begins to lose interest in a book, ask her questions you know she can answer. For example, if your child is already counting out loud and enjoys counting, you can ask her questions such as, "How many bunnies are on the page?" and then ask her to go through the page, count up the number of bunnies, and shout out the answer.

The same thing could work with colors. If your child likes colors, you can ask her to name all of the colors she sees on a page.

STEP 2:

Once you have your child's attention again, you can ask her more detailed questions about the story or about certain words you're reading. Then continue reading the story.

Questions you may ask about the story include:
• How do you feel about what's happening here?
• What do you think will happen next?
• What do you think about [name a character]? Why do you feel that way?

Helping Your Child See Himself or Herself as a Growing Reader

WHEN TO USE THIS ACTIVITY:

Consider using this activity if your young child has tearfully told you, "I can't read" or is just frustrated that he cannot read yet. While he may not be able to read all the words in a book, remind him that it's important that he understands that he is building upon and learning important skills that lead to reading. This activity contains some discussion points you can use with your child that will hopefully encourage him to see himself as a successful growing reader.

STEP 1:

Growing readers are learning their letters and numbers.

Some young children are unaware that learning how to read is a **process**—instead, they just expect to pick up a book one day and magically be able to read it. If your child is still learning his letters and numbers, you can say, "Right now, you're reading letters. Did you know that readers learn how to read by learning their letters first? You're doing that, and I know that one day we'll be putting those letters together to make words. Then you'll learn those words, and WOW, you'll be reading words!"

Also consider telling your child of a time it took you a long time to learn something (it could even be reading). Share that while it was sometimes frustrating to not just know how to do that thing right away, you practiced and eventually learned how to do that thing well.

STEP 2:

Growing readers already know a few words, whether they know it or not!

Thanks to universal traffic signs and advertisement logos, many young children already know some words by sight, even though they haven't mastered all the sounds. Some of these include:

- a STOP sign
- a GO sign
- an EXIT sign
- grocery store signs
- restaurant signs

You can tell your child, "I notice that you already know some everyday words, words that you see around you. That's terrific! When you recognize a word, you're reading! Next time we're in

(continued on following page)

the car, you should call out those words you see." If you ever run into any of these signs with your child, be sure to take advantage of this teachable moment and ask your child to read it for you. For example, if you're passing by an EXIT sign, you might say, "Do you know what that green sign says?" If your child doesn't know what it says, you might say, "It says EXIT: this sign means that this is one of the doors you can use to leave or exit the building. How many letters are in the word EXIT? Let's count them. What's the first letter in EXIT? Yes, it's an 'e' which makes an /e/ sound. What's the last letter in EXIT? Yes, it's a 't' which makes a /t/ sound."

STEP 3:
Growing readers can follow along with familiar songs and poems, even if they don't know all the words.

You'd be surprised how well growing readers can learn to track their finger to the lyrics of "Happy Birthday to You." Why? Because they already know the words to the song! While this task may appear to be "fake reading" in the sense that your child is not decoding the words, tracking (or following) familiar songs and poems certainly gives young children an awareness of print (reading from left to right) and the segmentation of words (it's not "happybirthdaytoyou"). By building familiar texts such as this song with your child, you'll give him confidence to read. You'll also give him golden opportunities to begin recognizing individual words.

STEP 4:
Growing readers already know how to read pictures and illustrations to gain comprehension.

If your child says, "I can't read, I only read baby books," tell him, "Do you mean picture books? Picture books aren't just for babies. Older kids read picture books too. I read picture books, in fact, I like reading picture books! Did you know that good readers read the pictures just as much as they read the words on the page? You can learn a lot about a book by reading the pictures – how characters are moving, how characters are feeling, what's going on in the story. I notice that you look at pictures in a book to figure out what's going on. That's great! When you start reading words, don't stop reading the pictures. It's an important thing to do!"

STEP 5:
Growing readers can enjoy listening to and appreciating a good book.

The more a young child can enjoy a good story, the more likely he will see himself as a reader and lover of books. Growing readers are not only learning the mechanics of letters and words; they are also gaining an appreciation for storytelling and different kinds of literature. They are learning that there are different kinds of stories (or genres) like fairy tales, and animal folktales. While your child may not yet be able to read an entire book by himself, he will probably be able to tell you what his favorite story is.

So if your child loves *Clifford the Big Red Dog*, by all means, try to find a number of Clifford books for him to read. If you read those books to him, read them with a ton of expression to make them come alive. An interest in a certain story character or book series may provide the right kind of motivation your child needs to stay interested in reading!

The Talking Bag, page 13

Understanding What You're Reading Together

The Talking Bag

STEP 1:

Select a book you recently read with your child.

STEP 2:

Create or find items for your Talking Bag.

You don't have to be fancy here. You can even trace illustrations from the book, cut them out and place those in the bag. You can also use plastic figurines or cut outs from old magazines or newspapers.

STEP 3:

Use the Talking Bag with your child.

Here are a number of ways you can use the Talking Bag. Take advantage of opportunities to pull out objects from the Talking Bag and interact with your child during these activities.

Ask your child to use it to retell a story.
Encourage your child to take out certain items from the Talking Bag as she retells the story. For example, if the story is "Goldilocks and the Three Bears" (for a copy of this story, see page 7), your child might pull out a doll from the Talking Bag when Goldilocks talks. You may pull out the Bear and talk with "Goldilocks."

Ask your child to use it to retell her favorite scene in a story.
Encourage your child to browse through the book and to identify her favorite scene. Have your child retell that scene while using objects from the bag. She can do so in third person (playing a narrator's role) or by playing all of the characters.

(continued on following page)

Ask your child to use the Talking Bag to retell the story or a scene from the story, but to add a different ending.

Ask your child if she liked how the story (or a scene from the story) ended. Encourage her to come up with alternative endings to the story or scene and tell them using Talking Bag items.

Ask your child to tell an entirely new story.

Using the same items in the Talking Bag, encourage your child to tell an entirely different story. Have fun!

If you've adopted a child whose primary language is not English and is just learning English: If your child is unable to retell any part of the story, encourage her to use the Talking Bag items to reenact the story by manipulating the objects without or with limited talking.

Read it Again!

ACTIVITY 1:

Play "Find that Word" to help build your child's sight word vocabulary.

After your child has finished reading a familiar text, select a page and ask her to locate one particular word from a sentence.

Say: "Can you find the word 'run' in this sentence? What letter does 'run' start with? How do you know this word is 'run'? Now, let's read that entire sentence [that contains 'run'] again."

ACTIVITY 2:

Check your child's comprehension by asking her to retell the story in her own words.

Say: "I enjoyed re-reading this story! Let's close the book now. Tell me what happened in the story, starting from the beginning."

If your child cannot recall anything from the text, it's possible that the text is too challenging for her right now. Try re-reading the story again soon, but next time, stop after every few pages and discuss what's going on; ask, "What do you think about what just happened?" When you reach the end of the story this time, ask your child if she can re-tell the story to you. If your child still struggles, allow her to look at the illustrations to help out. Later, help her select a more appropriate text.

ACTIVITY 3:

Build your child's appreciation for literature by discussing your favorite parts of the text.

Ask: "That was a great poem! What's your favorite line? What's your favorite illustration? What does it make you think of? Here's my favorite part..."

Play-Act a Story

STEP 1:

After reading a story, encourage your child to retell it by "play-acting" or re-enacting the story.

For example, if you read Kevin Henkes' book, *Chrysanthemum* with your child, you would say: "Let's act out our favorite parts of *Chrysanthemum*!"

STEP 2:

As you prepare your retelling, decide with your child which part of the book to re-enact by reviewing both the words and the illustrations of the book.

Say: "Let's look through the book. What's your favorite part of the book? Why is that your favorite part? Which part should we act out? How should we act it out?"

STEP 3:

As you "play-act" your story, remind your child to act out the characters by remembering what they said and how they were portrayed in the illustrations. Try to include dialogue from the story.

Again, if you were working with the book *Chrysanthemum*, you could provide this example for your child: "I'm Victoria from the story. I'll have to remember to hold up my nose and say in a whiny voice, 'She's only named after a *flower*.'"

STEP 4:

Always applaud the efforts of your child after he re-enacts the story. Your enthusiasm and creativity may inspire him to appreciate the story even more. Don't be surprised if he wants to go back and revisit the same book later!

Turn and Talk

STEP 1:

As you read the book aloud, stop every few pages to "turn and talk" (respond) about what is going on in the story.

Pause at important places throughout the story to discuss the following open-ended questions with your child:

• "What do you think about what just happened?"
• "What do you think will happen next?"
• "What does this part of the story remind you of?"
• "How is the character feeling now?"

STEP 2:

If and when appropriate, you may want to briefly pause before the climax of a story to ask your child for predictions of what will happen next.

Remind your child that the goal of predicting is not to guess exactly what will happen, but to enjoy the story as it unfolds and changes. It's completely fine to not make accurate predictions.

STEP 3:

After you've finished reading the entire picture book, ask your child to share or draw about her favorite part or character in the book.

This activity allows your child to identify key themes and events from the story. After your child has captured her favorite part of the story on paper, encourage her to share it with other friends and family.

Using Tangible, Visual Items to Help with Reading Comprehension

ACTIVITY:

Even the best book illustrations do not always help children fully grasp what a book is discussing. When you read about new objects with your child, get some of those objects so that your child can touch and smell them and get a better understanding of what he's reading about.

Likewise, when you read about new places, you can bring out a map and pictures of the place to connect a geographic location to its literary context. This simple activity will lead your child to be much more engaged in what you're reading about.

If you'd like to play a game around any new objects you'll be reading about, think about doing the following:

LEARN-AT-HOME EXTENSION ACTIVITIES

- Tell your child that you're going to read about something new today called a _____. Show him a picture of the object in the book and then tell him that you've hid that object someplace in the room and that you'd like him to find it. Once your child finds the object, cheer and ask him what he thinks about it and what he thinks it's for or what it does.

- When you read about that new object in the story, put the object in one of your hands and make a fist with both hands (hiding the object). Tell your child that you have that object in one of your hands, and that he should guess which one it's in.

Things I Like, page 22

How Print Works
(Concepts of Print)

Learning that Sounds in Words Can be Written with Letters

STEP 1:

Say, "I'm going to say three words that begin with the same sound. Listen carefully: dog, day, and dance. Dog, day, and dance [emphasize the beginning sound]. All three of these words begin with the same sound, /d/. Dog, day, and dance."

STEP 2:

Now, tell your child that you are going to say another word and that you want her to think about whether or not it begins like dog, day and dance:

Say, "I'm going to say another word and I want you to listen and tell me whether or not you think this word begins like dog, day, and dance. The word I am thinking of is **dark**. Does **dark** begin like dog, day, and dance? [Wait for your child to respond.] Yes, it does! Now, I'm going to give you another word and I want you to tell me whether or not you think it begins like dog, day, and dance. Listen: dog, day, dance, and **dive**. Does **dive** start like the other words?" [Invite your child to respond.]

Repeat this exercise with other words, such as dive, deep, and door, always using "D" words. After doing this a few times, invite your child to give new words. After a while, try one or two words that do not begin with the /d/ sound. Repeat this step as often as you like.

STEP 3:

Now explain that these sounds are also letters.

Say, "We know that the words dog, day, and dance **sound** the same at the beginning. I wonder what they each **look like** at the beginning. I'm going to write them down so we can find out." [Write the words dog, day and dance on paper. Invite your child to "read" the words with you, pointing to each word as you say them.]

(continued on following page)

Ask, "What do you notice about the beginning of each of these words? [Invite your child to respond.] That's right, all three words look the same at the beginning! All three words share the same beginning letter, and that letter is the letter **D**. Dog, day, and dance all begin with the letter **D**, which makes a /d/ sound." Underline the **D** of each word so that your child sees the similarities.

STEP 4:

It's important that you introduce only one letter and its corresponding sound at a time. Remember that the goal of this activity reaches beyond learning about the sound-letter relationship of /d/. The larger goal is to help your child understand that sounds in words can be written with letters.

Things I Like
Learning that Words are Symbols for Real Things

WHEN TO USE THIS ACTIVITY:

It's important for children to learn early on that speech can be written down. This knowledge will support your child's understanding of what a "word" is (what the beginning and ending of words look like and the visual order of letters within a word), and will help your child understand what letters are (letters have distinct shapes, have names, and form words). Use this activity to help foster your child's understanding of this important concept.

MATERIALS

• Appropriate magazines

• Paper (not ruled)

• Scissors

• Glue or paste

STEP 1:

Prepare a supply of pictures cut from magazines or other sources.

STEP 2:

Print the words "Things I Like" at the top of the piece of paper. Ask your child to select three pictures of things she likes. These pictures may follow a theme, such as "Toys I Like" or "Animals I Like." Help her paste the pictures on her paper.

STEP 3:

Encourage your child to name aloud the item in the pictures she chose. Write the name of each item below its picture, saying aloud the letters as you write. These words should be written in all lowercase letters, except when it is a proper noun.

Use this opportunity to help develop your child's vocabulary. If your child offers a correct word other than the word you expect, you might ask, "This thing has more than one name, can you think of it?" If your child doesn't know what you're thinking of, say the word. Definitely do not overwhelm your child by providing too many alternative words.

If your child is not seeing the connection between the words you write and the pictures, point out that symbols stand for things. For example, touch the table both of you are at and say, "This is a real table that you're touching right now." Then show the picture of the table your child selected and say, "Here's a picture of a table." Now write the word table and say, "This is the word that stands for table, and we can read it and write it. This is the word table."

(continued on following page)

STEP 4:

After you have finished writing, read the words again, pointing to each word. Encourage your child to "read" these words **with** you. As your child reads with you, observe her ability to recognize words and letters. As she matches words to pictures, prompt her to look at all the letters (not just the first one) to begin to understand that all the letters make up that particular word.

If you've adopted a child whose primary language is not English and is just learning English: Whenever possible, find out what something is called in your child's home language and write the word in both English and her home language. If you do not know the correct spelling of the word, do not attempt to write it; just have your child say the word for you in her home language.

Learning to Write and Recognize Your Name

ACTIVITY 1:

Make up short rhyming poems or songs that include your child's name, then sing it together.

Spell out his name in a simple tune, a rhythmic chant, or a cheer while showing him the letters: "Give me a **D**! Give me an **I**! Give me an **O**! Give me an **N**! What does that spell? **DION**!"

ACTIVITY 2:

Print your child's name on two index cards, then cut apart the letters on the second card. Help your child reconstruct the letters to match the uncut card.

ACTIVITY 3:

Help your child trace letters with his index finger in a sandbox or in shaving or whipped cream spread across foil or newspaper. To keep things more clean, you could also help your child form letters using Play-Doh® or pipe cleaners. Once he can form the letters nice and large, encourage him to try practicing on paper with pencils.

ACTIVITY 4:

Help your child find the letters of his name in a collection of letter cards, letter magnets, or in a piece of appropriate text that has large-sized printing.

ACTIVITY 5:

Model for your child how you print all the letters in his name, saying the letter names as you go.

Explain how the letters you print stand for the sounds in the name: "**D** is the /d/ sound at the beginning, then **i** makes the /i/ sound. Next comes the **o** with the /o/ sound..."

Word Searching at Home

STEP 1:

Say, "I'm going to show you a special word that is somewhere else in the room. It is the word **Sunday**. I'll spell it." After you say that, print the word in large letters on a 5 by 7 inch index card. Say each letter out loud as you write the word. After you've written the word, say the word once again.

NOTE: Try to select words that are relevant to your child, like familiar names and words that are featured over and over again in books you read together.

STEP 2:

Ask, "Let's try to find the word **Sunday** in the room." Use prompts to help your child think critically such as, "Where do you think we can find that word in this room?"

STEP 3:

Give your child a copy of the special word on a 5 by 7 inch index card to hold, and ask him to search for that same special word somewhere in the room.

When your child has found the special word, help him check to see if he is right. Say, "Let's spell the word to check if it is the same word. Let's look at the first letter. What letter is it? That's right, it's the letter **S**. Do both words start with the letter **S**?" Continue with the following letters until you all agree that the words are indeed the same.

STEP 4:

Repeat this word search with one or two more words. Also, after your child has found other words, notice whether or not your child pays attention to letters that follow the first letter when two words begin with the same letter. For example, you might ask, "You found **Sunday**, great job! How come you didn't match the special word to **Saturday**? They both begin with an **S**. What else did you look for?"

(continued on following page)

STEP 5:

After each special word is found, talk about how that word is useful in your child's everyday life: "The word **Sunday** is one of the days of the week on our calendar. The word **Sunday** helps us know that it is a certain day in our week."

STEP 6:

As your child learns more about letters and words, challenge him to try this game by looking at the word cards once but not taking it with him on his search. (If your child ends up needing the card, definitely give it to him.) After he has found the special word, hand him the word card to double-check it. This activity then doubles as a visual memory game.

OUT-AND-ABOUT
**EXTENSION
ACTIVITY**

Consider keeping a stack of short words in the car. When you're driving, hand your child a card and ask him to find that word.

Zany Reading

> ## WHEN TO USE THIS ACTIVITY:
> Play this game to see if your child has mastered her knowledge about how text and books work (such as knowing that we read English from left to right and that we read books from front to back). Understanding of these concepts grows out of being read to and having other experiences with books and text.

STEP 1:

Hold the book upside down. Ask your child, "Is this the right way to hold our book? It isn't? How come? Show me the right way to hold it."

STEP 2:

Read a line from right to left, pointing with your finger. Ask, "What? You think I'm reading backward? Then which direction should I read?"

STEP 3:

Look at the book illustrations and as you point to images on the page say, for example, "Red hen, blue sky, green leaves. [Your child may point out that you're doing something wrong.] What? I'm reading the pictures. Isn't that what I'm supposed to read? I'm supposed to read the words, not the pictures? Which word should I read first? Should I start reading the last word on the page? How about starting with a word in the middle of the page? Which word would you like me to read? The first word on the page? Okay, that sounds right, let's do it!"

STEP 4:

Read lines backward, from bottom to top, from back to front—whatever it takes to cause your child to catch your zany reading. Laugh and have her show you how to do it appropriately.

NOTE:

If your child doesn't recognize your intentional mistakes, be more explicit by pausing and asking questions such as, "Is this making sense to you? Hmmm, something doesn't seem right. Maybe I shouldn't be reading backwards. What do you think? What direction should I be reading?"

Create Your Own Menu, page 38

Learning About Books & Other Forms of Text

Taking Care of Books

STEP 1:

Have clean hands before reading a book.

You can say, "One way to take care of a book is to make sure our hands are clean before reading. If our hands are dirty, we leave fingerprints and smudges on the pages. If our hands are clean, we keep the pages clean."

STEP 2:

Remember to turn pages carefully, from the top.

Turning pages with one's thumb and index finger from the top right hand corner of the page does not always come naturally, but your child can learn with your help. Ask your child to watch you turn the pages of a book and ask her what she notices. You might say, "One way we can take care of books is to turn pages carefully, from the top right hand corner. I will turn the pages and I want you to watch me. What did you see me doing? Can you show me how you turn the pages of a book?"

STEP 3:

Never write, scribble, glue, or cut the pages of your book.

Many young children are familiar with writing and drawing in coloring books, so it's important to help your child distinguish between coloring/activity books and reading books. Explain to your child, "Certain books are meant to be read over and over again. [Take out a book you're reading.] What would happen if I cut a page out of this book and you wanted to read it? How would you feel? [Wait for your child's response and, if you think it's necessary, discuss how people need to think of others who will read the same book in the future.] Since we read these books over and over again, and because others will read them, it's important that the books stay clean and are kept in the same condition in which we find them. The only thing that

(continued on following page)

belongs on these book pages are our clean fingers, not crayons, scissors or glue. We **can** use crayons, scissors and glue in our coloring books. [Show your child a coloring book.]"

STEP 4:

Save your place with a bookmark, not by folding a page or laying a book face down.

Introduce this practice of caring for books by making bookmarks with your child (see page 173 for bookmark templates you can cut out and color). Then discuss the purpose of bookmarks with your child: "How do readers use bookmarks? How are bookmarks helpful?" Explain that using a bookmark is one way to take care of books: "If we want to keep our place in a book, a bookmark does the job for us. I could keep my place by folding a page or laying the book face down, but our book would get pretty worn out. Using a bookmark helps keep our book in good shape."

STEP 5:

Put your book in a safe place at home, away from babies and pets.

Talk about the safe places where you store books at home. You might say, "Babies and pets sometimes like to chew books or rip their pages, so remember to put your books where [pet's name] and [baby's name] can't reach them. What are some safe places to put your books? Where are some unsafe places to put your books?"

LEARN-AT-HOME EXTENSION ACTIVITY   Ask your child to explain how to turn pages to a sibling, another adult, a pet (many young kids love reading to and teaching dogs), or to her favorite doll or stuffed animal.

LEARN-AT-HOME EXTENSION ACTIVITY   Make one or more bookmarks with your child using construction paper, markers, crayons and stickers. Perhaps your child will use the bookmark you make in her books, and you'll use the bookmark she makes in your books. Page 173 has bookmark templates that you can cut out and use.

Making a "Caring for My Books" Book

WHEN TO USE THIS ACTIVITY:

Your child is going to learn to care for books by making his own book called, *Caring for My Books*.

MATERIALS

- The *Caring for My Books* book on page 175
- Scissors
- Stapler
- Crayons or markers

STEP 1:

Cut out the pages for the mini book and staple the pages together.

STEP 2:

Read the book with your child. Each page contains advice on how to care for books. Ask your child questions about book care, such as:

- What do we do before we pick up a book to read it?
- Do we turn the pages of our books quickly or slowly?
- Can you show me how we turn the pages?
- What do we do after we finish reading a book?

STEP 3:

Illustrate your book together with crayons or markers. With the illustrations, your child will be able to revisit and think about the book's meaning, even if he cannot yet read its text.

Learning How Books Work

WHEN TO USE THIS ACTIVITY:

Use this activity to determine whether your child knows his or her concepts of print (one's knowledge of the various parts of a book and how they work) such as:

- The purpose of a book title;
- The direction in which we read (left to right & top to bottom);
- What illustrations tell us and how we use them.

MATERIALS

- Two or three picture books with one to two lines of text on each page (not ABC books or picture dictionaries)

STEP 1:

Sit side-by-side with your child and ask, "What have we read lately? What did you like about what we read?"

STEP 2:

Show your child the books you selected. Ask something like, "I'd love for you to read some pictures to me. Which book do you want to start with?"

STEP 3:

Once your child selects a book, place the closed book in her hands. Ask: "Before we read this, can you show me the front of the book?" Then ask, "How about the back of the book?"

Next, track the book's title with your index finger, reading the title aloud to your child. Still keeping the book closed, discuss: "What do you think this story will be about?" Then, "How does the title help us know that?" Then, "How do the pictures on the cover help us know what the book will be about?"

The key here is to find out if your child understands the function of a book title and cover illustrations and to teach her about what these things do if she doesn't already know.

(continued on following page)

STEP 4:

Next, ask your child to look ONLY through the illustrations of the book before reading the actual lines of text (this is also known as a "picture walk"). Say: "We're not going to read the words just yet. Tell me the story using the pictures."

STEP 5:

Read the text to your child, putting your finger under each word. Explain that we read from the left to right and from the top of the page to the bottom.

STEP 6:

If your child doesn't demonstrate an understanding of how print works described in Steps 1 through 5, choose ONE of these concepts to introduce and teach to your child. Save the other concepts for later. Introducing too many at a time can overwhelm a child.

As you do this, observe the following: Does she know that a book begins from beginning to end, or does she just randomly flip pages? How well does she understand and follow the story line?

If you've adopted a child whose primary language is not English and is just learning English: It is important to keep in mind that your child's home language may be written in very different ways than the English language. For example, some languages are read from right to left, or from top to bottom where symbolic characters are read vertically. As you introduce the directionalilty of English print to your child, point out these differences, but avoid statements that place a value on those differences. For example, you can say, "In English, we read from left to right," but do not say, "We read from left to right; reading from right to left is the WRONG way to read." Statements like that can lead your child to feel that you are placing a negative value on her home language.

My ABC Book

WHEN TO USE THIS ACTIVITY:

Use this activity to help your child construct his own ABC book so that he can begin writing while he learns his letters. At the end of this project, he will have a book that he can read every page of by himself.

MATERIALS

- Paper (any kind), standard size, cut into 28 half sheets
- Pictures from books or flashcards
- Markers or crayons
- Staples (or anything to bind the book once it's done)

STEP 1:

On each half sheet of paper, write the capital and lowercase form of one letter of the alphabet. You could also write dotted lines of the letters for your child to trace, or allow him to write the letters on his own. Next to the letter write "is for" and leave a blank space for a picture.

STEP 2:

Beginning with the "A" page, ask your child if he knows of something that starts with each letter. If he doesn't, look at books, magazines, or the Alphabet Letter and Picture Sheets on page 99 to give your child ideas.

Once your child names an object, he can finish the page by drawing that object on her own or with you. You or your child can also write the name of that object.

STEP 3:

After your child finishes each page, ask him to read the completed page to you, pointing to each word (or letter or picture) as he says it. The first couple of times you read, you may need to help your child with reading "is for."

Continue with these steps for each letter of the alphabet, encouraging your child to become more independent as you go on. Soon, your child will be reading each page without difficulty.

(continued on following page)

STEP 4:

Finally, help your child make a front and back cover for his book with the two remaining sheets of paper. Come up with a title such as "My ABC Book" or "(Child's Name)'s ABC Book."

Stack the sheets together and staple them along the left edge, or use another creative way to bind them together.

Now your child has a book that he wrote and can practice reading with all on his own.

Create Your Own Menu

STEP 1:

Discuss the purpose of menus at restaurants.

You may say something like, "Have you ever seen a menu? What does a menu look like? Who uses a menu? Where do you use a menu? How do you use a menu?"

Help familiarize your child with menus by showing him the samples you collected.

STEP 2:

Tell your child that you're going to work together to create a menu for a restaurant today.

Flip through some magazines with your child and cut out pictures of any foods he wants to serve at his restaurant. Let your child's imagination run wild; if he wants his restaurant to serve imaginary kinds of food or mixtures of cuisines, that's fine.

STEP 3:

Help your child fold a piece of construction paper in half to create a "menu."

Now your child can paste the pictures in his menu. Depending on where your child is in his development, he may be able to write names, descriptions and prices next to the photos. If your child isn't ready to write, ask him to think of the first sound or letter he hears for each food word. Then write or help your child write those words next to the pictures.

(continued on following page)

STEP 4:

Ask your child to think of a name for his restaurant and to write that name on the cover of the menu (you may need to help your child write the name).

If your child is having a tough time coming up with a name, you can share one or more of these examples:
• Nick's Noodles
• Beyonce's Burgers
• Penny's Pizza Parlor
• Farrah's Fancy Foods
• Rosa's Royal Restaurant

STEP 5:

Put your child's menu to work!

Have fun playing restaurant, ordering from your child's menu. Help your child point out any words and prices in his menu by including it in your dialogue as you play along:
• So tell me, how much are your hamburgers?
• Where are the hamburgers listed in this menu?
• What letter does hamburger start with again?

Letter Fishing, page 42

Recognizing the Letters of the Alphabet

Alphabet Aerobics

STEP 1:

Select one or more of the Alphabet Letter and Picture Sheets to work on today.

STEP 2:

For each sheet, ask your child to say the names of each letter with you.

STEP 3:

Encourage your child to act out one or more of the pictures that go along with the letter. You can act out one of the pictures as well. While your child is acting, make the sound of each letter together. So for the letter **C**, your child can pretend to drive a **car** and you'll make the sound for **C** together.

STEP 4:

Now ask your child to trace the shape of the letter in the air as **big** as she can. Make the sound of the letter with your child as she traces it. If she can't remember how to make a letter, let her trace it with a pencil on the Letter and Picture Sheet, and also guide her hand as you help her trace the letter in the air.

Three Games to Play with Letter Cut-outs

> **WHEN TO USE THESE ACTIVITIES:**
> Play these games to give your child additional practice in recognizing the letters of the alphabet.
>
> **MATERIALS**
> • Alphabet Fish Cut-outs on page 125
> • Optional (for Letter Fishing): paper clips; magnet; stick; piece of string

GRAB BAG

Place the Alphabet Fish Cut-outs in a bag. Ask your child to close his eyes, choose a letter, open his eyes, and then say what it is and the sound it makes. Help your child think of words that begin with each letter. If your child doesn't name the correct letter or say the correct sound, tell him what it is and return the fish to the bag.

LETTER SEARCH

Scatter the Alphabet Fish Cut-outs face up on a flat surface and ask your child to find a specific letter. Say, for example, "Okay, find the letter C!" If your child selects an incorrect letter, locate the correct letter so that your child can visualize it. Make each selected letter's sound(s) together, and together, think of words that begin with that letter. You can refer to the Alphabet Letter and Picture Sheets on page 99 to see pictures of words that begin with each letter.

LETTER FISHING

Take the stick and attach a string and a magnet at the end of the string. Next, attach a paperclip to each fish.

Scatter the cut-outs on the ground or on your table, hand your child the "fishing pole" and ask your child to fish for specific letters. After catching each letter, ask him to say the letter's sound(s) and together, think of words that begin with the letter.

A Skywriting Adventure

WHEN TO USE THIS ACTIVITY:

This quick, engaging game will help your child learn to recognize her letters, and can be especially useful if your child confuses some letters with others (e.g., mistaking b's for d's).

MATERIALS

- Post-it® notes or small pieces of paper
- The *Serena the Skywriter* story on page 44
- Optional: plain paper and crayons

STEP 1:

Prepare for your skywriting adventure.

Choose one or two letters your child finds challenging to write or identify. If you select one letter, write that letter on ten small pieces of paper. If you choose two letters, write each letter on five pieces of paper.

If you'd like, you can write a letter your child knows well on other pieces of paper.

STEP 2:

Play the game.

Tell your child that she's going to search for specific letters, and that she needs to find a certain number of each specific letter. Show your child the letters she'll look for and review their names. If your child is learning the letters' sounds, you can also review their sounds.

Use the "Serena the Skywriter" story and instructions on the next page to conduct the search. If your child needs help identifying the letters during the game, definitely help your child out.

STEP 3:

After your child captures her letters, ask her to think about words that begin with the letters she found and to tell you those words. Write down those words for her so that she can see her letters being used. You can also ask your child to draw pictures of the words she comes up with.

Hello there!

My name is Serena the Skywriter. I'm the fastest, most daring skywriting pilot in the air.

I flew all the way to you today because I really, really, really need your help.

You see, I've been skywriting letters for a long time today. Though I may be the fastest skywriting pilot around, all of those looping twists and turns I do to write the letters make me so dizzy. I'm so dizzy that I can't look up at the sky to make sure I wrote the correct letters!

I need you to help me search the sky for my letters and let me know if I wrote them correctly. In fact, I want you to keep a special look out for the letter ____. I really don't think I wrote that one too well today.

When you find a letter, all you have to do is put your finger on it for five seconds, repeating the name of the letter over and over again.

After you catch 10 ___'s, sky write that letter in the air using your pointer finger. Just don't get dizzy like me!

Thanks so much for your help!

Your high-flying friend,

Serena the Skywriter

Alphabet Letters and Sharks

STEP 1:

Spread a select number of the Alphabet Fish Cut-outs on the floor so that your child can see all of the letters from any one point. Use between six and eight letters at a time.

Tape the cards to the floor to prevent your child from slipping on them during the game.

STEP 2:

Start the game by describing the situation to your child: Both of you are going to "swim" around the ocean (by walking around the cards and making swimming gestures with your arms), and when you see a shark, you'll call out "Shark!" to your child. Both of you will become "safe" by standing on a letter and calling out the letter's name. If your child is learning his letter sounds, both of you can also say the sound your respective letters make. If your child has mastered all of the letters' names and sounds, challenge him to call out one word that begins with the letter he's standing on. If your child names a letter incorrectly, make sure you provide the correct answer so he will become more familiar with that letter.

LEARN-AT-HOME EXTENSION ACTIVITY Did you know that most sharks actually aren't dangerous to people? If your child is interested in sharks, consider downloading information and activities to share together from the Monterey Bay Aquarium at http://www.mbayaq.org/efc/sharks.asp. The site contains fascinating facts about sharks, stories of how different cultures think about sharks, and a wealth of arts and crafts activities for children.

Alphabet Safari
Discovering Letter Formations in Your Community

WHEN TO USE THIS ACTIVITY:

Help your child identify letters and discover that letters are all around her by taking an outdoor "Alphabet Safari." You can take an "Alphabet Safari" any time you go for a walk or drive.

MATERIALS

- Pencils and a portable writing surface for your child to write on when she goes outside (such as a clipboard or a notebook)
- Optional: a still camera

STEP 1:

Share with your child examples or pictures of how letters can be found in indoor and outdoor settings.

Here are some examples:

The letter "O" can be found on a manhole cover.

The uppercase letter "A" can be found on the side of a ladder.

The letter "v" can be seen upside-down on some a-framed rooftops.

STEP 2:

After sharing a few examples of hidden letters, take your child on an "Alphabet Safari."

Find hidden letters on buildings, parks, trash cans, and other outside objects. Ask your child to draw or sketch the letters she sees.

STEP 3:

After your safari, have your child share her findings. Compile your child's sketches to make an "Alphabet Safari" book!

(continued on following page)

If You Cannot Take Your Child Outside for a Safari:

Conduct a safari inside your home or take pictures of various letter formations in your community, print those pictures, and have your child hunt for letter formations in the pictures. You can also look through magazines or search the Internet for pictures of cities, towns and other places.

LEARN-AT-HOME EXTENSION ACTIVITY	Play a "Hide and Seek" version of this game by telling your child, "In the kitchen, there's the letter L made out of two straws. Go try to find it." Your child can then look for formations in a certain room of the house and ask you to find those items. You and your child can give each other pointers by telling each other that you're "warm" or "cold" as you get closer and further from the items.
OUT-AND-ABOUT EXTENSION ACTIVITY	You and your child can discover letter formations anywhere you go – while you're driving, while standing in line, or while taking a walk. Spend a few minutes searching for letter formations with your child every now and then. You may decide to keep track of how many formations each of you see (a great game for siblings to play with one another).

Alphabet Dice

STEP 1:

Make the game pieces.

Cut two half-gallon milk cartons in half. Push one carton bottom inside the other to form a large cube. Do this again with the other two cartons to form the second die. Write the capital letters you want to practice on the various sides of the dice. More than one side of a die can have the same letter.

STEP 2:

Play the game.

Ask your child to roll the dice and then name the letters that each die stops on.

Encourage her to also make the sound of that letter or to think of a word that begins with that letter. (Both of you can refer to the Alphabet Letter and Picture Sheets on page 99.) You should also take turns rolling the dice and modeling what you'd like her to do with the letters.

STEP 3:

Ask her to draw the lower case letter that matches the capital letter on a piece of paper. If you think you'll find it helpful, you can use the Alphabet Letter Formation Motion sheets on pages 94 and 95.

STEP 4:

When your child finishes writing the matching lower case letters, have her repeat which letters she rolled and then wrote.

Make Your Bed
Distinguishing Between Lowercase "b" and "d"

STEP 1:

Before doing this with your child, take a moment to place both of your hands in a fist with thumbs pointing up. The knuckles on your right hand should touch those on the left, and the inside of your thumbs should face each other. This should resemble a bed.

STEP 2:

Now, ask your child to watch you "make a bed" with your hands.

STEP 3:

Tell your child that this is a bed, and ask him to identify what letter the word "bed" starts with.

STEP 4:

Show your child the lowercase "b" and "d" at the bottom of this page.

Placing your hands in the "bed" position, ask your child which letter at the bottom of this page looks more like the first part of the bed (going from left to right). He should match it with the "b."

STEP 5:

Now ask him which letter at the bottom of this page looks more like the end of the bed (your right hand). He should match it with the "d."

STEP 6:

Encourage your child, saying that anytime he gets stuck trying to remember if a letter is a "b" or "d," he can always make a bed, matching up the letters he reads to his own hands.

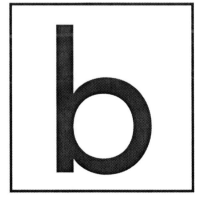

When Children Think "L, M, N, O & P" Are One Letter

WHEN TO USE THIS ACTIVITY:

Use this activity if your child thinks that the letters L, M, N, O and P are actually ONE letter (a very common issue).

MATERIALS

* The alphabet song on page 53

STEP 1:

Sing the Alphabet Song with your child.

If your child is just learning the alphabet, you may have sung the "Alphabet Song" with her. Singing the Alphabet Song is one of the best ways to expose children to the alphabet.

STEP 2:

Help your child associate the alphabet song with printed letters.

After your child is familiar with the song, move onto the process of helping her associate the song with printed letters. You're going to sing the song with your child again, but this time, place a copy of the song in front of her, pointing to each letter as you sing it. This will not only allow you to model that text is written from left to right, but will give your child an opportunity to learn that there is a written counterpart for each letter sound. Soon, your child will see that the sounds "L-M-N-O-P" are actually associated with five different letters.

STEP 3:

Foster independence in reading the alphabet song.

After you have modeled tracking your finger from left to right as you sing and read the song, invite your child to try it out for herself. Remind her that tracking works best when one's finger is beneath the letters, not directly on top of letters. Pointing to each letter while singing it will help your child begin to recognize and read the letters.

Alphabet Song Lyrics

A - B - C - D

E - F - G - H - I

J - K - L - M - N

O - P - Q - R - S

T - U - V

W - X - Y - Z

Now I know my A - B - C's.
Next time won't you sing with me?

Playing "Store" to Learn Letter Sounds, page 60

Letters and Their Sounds

Alphabet Hide and Seek

STEP 1:

Take the three small paper bags and label each one with a letter that your child needs to learn with (for instance, A, B, and C).

STEP 2:

Clip pictures of objects out of a magazine that begin with those letters, such as an **a**irplane, a **b**ed, and a **c**ow. You can also use cut-outs from the Alphabet Letter and Picture Sheets on page 99 or small objects from around your home that start with those letters.

Tape the pictures to note cards and write the corresponding letter on the back of each card.

STEP 3:

Look at each of the pictures with your child and talk about what they are and which letter of the alphabet they begin with. Next, tell your child to cover his eyes while you "hide" the pictures around the room, placing or taping the pictures in low, easy to reach spots. If hiding the pictures around the room doesn't seem like a good idea, you can also scatter them on a table, the floor, or outside.

STEP 4:

Together, hunt for the pictures. When your child finds one, cheer and ask him to tell you what the object is, to name the letter it starts with, and to say the sound that letter makes (you can say the sound together). After he does this, ask him to toss the letter into the corresponding letter bag.

OUT-AND-ABOUT EXTENSION ACTIVITY

When you're out of the house on some days, decide with your child to hunt for objects that begin with a certain letter. When your child identifies those objects, let him take a picture of them. You can then print those pictures and make a collage or book of all of the objects in your community that begin with that letter.

Alphabet Basketball

STEP 1:

Make the basket.

On the plastic cup, draw a basketball net pattern with the black marker. With the note card or piece of cardboard, make a backboard with a colored square just above the cup's rim, and tape the card to the back of the cup.

STEP 2:

Set up the game.

Decide on the number of letters you'll work on today and cut out that number of basketballs from page 97. On the blank side of the balls, write one letter your child will practice. (The first time you play this game, start with one or two letters, and then gradually increase that number as you figure out how much time your child needs to learn the letters.)

STEP 3:

Play the game!

To start, lay out the basketballs with the letter side face down. You're going to ask your child to flip over the basketballs one at a time. When she names the correct letter, she can shoot a ball into the "net." If she does not name the letter correctly, just place the ball aside and say that you'll come back to that ball later. (For these letters, you might use some of the activities in the section called "Recognizing the Letters of the Alphabet," which begins on page 40).

(continued on following page)

Tell your child that when she makes a basket, both of you will pretend that the sound the ball makes is the sound of the letter that is on the back of the basketball. So when she shoots the basketball into the hoop, both of you should excitedly say the letter's sound. (You may need to give your child a few examples.)

Be sure to cheer on your child. You can even use cheers you hear at sporting events.

Using Pictures to Work on Letter/Sound Identification

STEP 1:

Take two pieces of construction paper and have your child draw a large P in the middle of one of the pieces. Do the same thing with the other sheet of paper but place a letter B in the middle.

STEP 2:

Cut out pictures that represent B and P sounds from a magazine or from the Alphabet Letter and Picture Sheets on page 99. For example, a picture of a bike would work for B and a picture of a pair of pants would work for P. Shuffle the pictures and place them in the envelope.

STEP 3:

Tell your child that he will be helping the pictures in the envelopes "find their home." Explain that each picture represents either a B sound or a P sound. Say, "Our job is to help these lost pictures find their correct letter and glue the pictures on the right pieces of paper to make sure they don't get lost again."

STEP 4:

Place the two sheets of paper with the letters in front of your child. Then have your child identify each picture in the envelope and decide which letter page to glue the picture onto. Have her name the letter and sound, and then ask her to glue the picture around the letter. Have your child draw an arrow from the picture to the target letter.

(continued on following page)

STEP 5:

Once your child has glued all of the pictures to the pages, recap what she's learned by asking her to point to and say the name of the picture, the corresponding letter, and the letter's sound.

Now the "lost pictures" have a home! Congratulate your child on working hard to make sure the pictures found their rightful home.

Playing "Store" to Learn Letter Sounds

WHEN TO USE THIS ACTIVITY:

Try out this activity with your child if he is just learning alphabet letters and the sounds they make. This activity will help him recognize his letter sounds through imaginative play with you.

MATERIALS

- Paper
- Scissors
- Crayons

STEP 1:

Set up your store.

You don't need elaborate props to play, just a great imagination. For example, a table or a large box can serve as a checkout stand, a bookcase can serve as a store shelf, and the store's goods can even be invisible.

STEP 2:

Tell your child that you'd like to play store with him.

You can say, "Charlie, let's play store for a little bit. We can pretend to work at our favorite store and sell anything you'd like. Who should be the customer first? Who should run the cash register first?"

STEP 3:

As you're playing, suggest to your child that you sell only things that begin with a certain letter sound.

Say, "Hey, I have an idea! Why don't we sell things that begin with the same letter sound? What letter sound should we choose?"

Let's say your child chooses the /b/ sound. Then say, "A /b/ [make the sound, don't say the letter] sound? What letter is that? That's right, it's the letter B! Do you know what B looks like?"

If your child doesn't know how to write the letter B, model it for him.

(continued on following page)

STEP 4:

Once you and your child have chosen a letter sound, draw pictures of things a store can sell that start with that letter. After coloring, you can cut out the pictures and use them to buy and sell. So for a store where everything starts with the /b/ sound, you could have pictures of things such as boots, balls, berries, blankets, and brushes.

STEP 5:

By engaging in imaginative play, you have an opportunity to invite your child to practice speaking in a context that is both meaningful and fun. In addition to the above steps, use this activity to engage your child in conversations at your store:

"Hello. How are you today?"

"What is your name? My name is..."

"I would like to buy a blanket. What kind of blankets do you have?"

"Goodbye. See you later."

If you've adopted a child whose primary language is not English and is just learning English: Your child may not be familiar with certain English words or phrases. If this is the case, think about referencing a particular word in your child's first language before introducing the English equivalent of the word. If you need help translating "store" words into your child's home language, you can do so by entering the word into free language translators on the Internet, such as the one at http://www.google.com/language_tools.

Playing With Puppets to Develop Listening and Speaking Skills , page 63

Developing Your Child's Listening and Speaking Skills

Playing With Puppets to Develop Listening and Speaking Skills

WHEN TO USE THIS ACTIVITY:

The more practice your child has to develop her listening and speaking skills, the better prepared she'll be to read and write. This activity presents you with a number of ways you can develop your child's listening and speaking skills by using finger puppets or stuffed animals.

MATERIALS

- One or more stuffed animals
- Optional: Puppet making materials (old gloves you can cut up, yarn, buttons, felt or similar materials, glue, scissors)

IDEA 1:

You and your child use the puppets or stuffed animals to talk with one another.

Here are some possible discussion topics:
- How was your day today?
- What did you eat for lunch today?
- What should we make for dinner tonight?
- Let's go on an imaginary trip today. Where do you want to go?
- Tell me about your favorite book.
- What's your favorite thing to do at the park?

You can also practice social interactions with your child. Here are some ideas:
- Imagine your puppets are friends and that they're walking down the street one day and run into each other. What should they say to each other when they meet?
- Imagine one stuffed animal is the new child in school or in a play group. How should the other puppets and stuffed animals interact with the new child?
- Imagine that the stuffed animals are friends, and that one of the stuffed animals is sad today. What can the other stuffed animal say to the sad one?

IDEA 2:

You and your child use the puppets or stuffed animals to tell stories or reenact scenes from your favorite books.

(continued on following page)

IDEA 3:

Ask your child to tell you and the stuffed animals or puppets a story (either make-believe or real).

Get creative, and in a different voice, use your puppet or stuffed animal to respond to your child's story. You can say things and ask questions such as:

- I really like this part of the story because it's funny. It makes me laugh!
- What did the dog look like? Was it a friendly dog?
- How did you feel when that happened to you?

Making Finger Puppets with Your Child

This activity presents a wonderful opportunity to make puppets with your child. You can make simple finger puppets by cutting the fingers off old gloves. Glue on felt face parts, yarn hair, or wiggle eyes from the craft store. Or make a puppet family by gluing a couple of eyes and a yarn mouth to each finger of a whole glove. You can also make a stick puppet of a favorite character from a book. Photocopy a picture of the character from the book, paste it onto cardboard (old cereal boxes work well), and attach a popsicle stick as a handle.

OUT-AND-ABOUT EXTENSION ACTIVITY

When you're in the car, bring one stuffed animal with you (you may need to explain to your child in advance that the stuffed animal will need to stay in the car once you get to where you're going). During the drive, tell your child that her stuffed animal would love to know what's going on, and that you'd like her to tell the stuffed animal what she sees, where they're going, and what she expects to do once both of you arrive at the destination. While this activity in and of itself offers great storytelling practice, you can explain directly that she is creating a story for her stuffed animal! This activity will reinforce her understanding of the importance of describing events and stories in chronological order.

I Spy a Rhyme

STEP 1:

The traditional "I Spy" game centers around one person trying to have another person guess a particular object based on clues that usually focus on the object's physical appearance. For example, someone picks an object in the room and says something like, "I spy something yellow," and others would name yellow objects in the room until someone guessed the correct object. "I Spy a Rhyme!," is played in a similar way, but with rhyming clues.

Here's an example: "I spy something that rhymes with **mat**."

MORE WAYS TO PLAY:

- Another way to play is to say the initial sound of a word [not the letter name]. So if you're looking at something that starts with an S, you'd say, "I spy something that starts with a 'ssss' sound."

- Ask your child to put words together: "I spy something that starts with a /b/ sound [say the sound, not the letter name] and ends with 'all.' What is it?"

If You Get Tired of Saying "I Spy"...

If you or your child gets tired of saying the words, "I spy," you can also say:
- *"I see something you don't see and it sounds like the word ____."*
- *"Somewhere in this room is a very special thing, and that thing starts with [say the letter sound]."*

- Your child may be ready to play by providing the answers in the form of a definition or by asking questions about what you see. In this game, if you're thinking of a hat when you tell your child, "I spy something that rhymes with mat," a great guess from him could be, "Is it something you put on your head?"

OUT-AND-ABOUT EXTENSION ACTIVITY

If you are out with your child, try playing this game in the car, while running errands, or while waiting for food at a restaurant. Take turns coming up with words of objects you see. Use any or all of the techniques above to provide hints to your child about the object you are thinking about.

What's In the Box?

WHEN TO USE THIS ACTIVITY:

This game is a fun way to encourage your child to practice listening and speaking skills in preparation for learning to read and write.

In this activity, one of you will describe a hidden mystery item to the other. The person who can't see the item will guess what it is.

MATERIALS

- Mystery items (toys, pieces of clothing, or healthy snacks)
- A box or dark bag big enough to hold one mystery item at a time
- A bag or pillowcase big enough to hold all of the mystery items

STEP 1:

Decide whether you or your child will be the clue-giver for this round of *What's In the Box?*

The clue-giver will tell the other person to close her eyes or face the opposite direction while the clue-giver takes one object from the pillowcase full of items and places it under a box or in the dark bag. After the clue-giver does this, she will tell the other person to open her eyes or to turn around.

STEP 2:

The clue-giver will try to describe the mystery item without naming it. For example, if the item is a toy car, she might say, "My mystery item has tires."

STEP 3:

After the clue-giver gives one hint, the other person is allowed to ask one yes-or-no type question that will help him identify the mystery item. Questions might include:
- "Does your mystery item have windows?"
- "Is your mystery item red?"
- "Does your mystery item have a big nose?"
- "Does your mystery item have a tail?"

STEP 4:

After the mystery item is identified, trade roles and repeat Steps 1 to 3. Play as many rounds as you want!

What Should We Talk About?
Building Your Child's Conversation Skills

WHEN TO USE THIS ACTIVITY:

The more your child participates in conversations, the easier of a time he or she will have learning to use the English language.

Here are some activities you can use to build your child's conversation skills. Your conversations may be about any topic, and you can have them anywhere – in the car, while waiting in line, while eating together, while taking a bath, or while getting ready for bed.

STEP 1:

Talk about activities and topics that interest your child.

Building your child's conversation skills should naturally develop from meaningful conversations with him. By allowing your child to share about things he is familiar and comfortable with, you allow him to talk with more confidence and ease.

Here are some topics or areas of interest that you and your child can talk and share about:

- Favorite games
- Favorite music artists
- Favorite songs
- Favorite sports
- Pictures of family and friends
- What happened at the park today
- What happened in play group today
- What he ate for lunch today
- What he did at school today
- Favorite cartoon/television characters
- Favorite movies
- Favorite books

You can begin conversations around these topics by saying, "Tell me about something you did at the park today" or "Can you tell me more about what you did with your brother today?" You could also ask, "Have I ever told you how much I love soccer? No? Well,..." When you're done talking, you can ask your child to tell you about his favorite sports or about something or somebody he loves.

STEP 2:

Invite your child to ask you questions.

Remember, conversation skills are not just about speaking, but also listening. Invite your child to learn about you by asking you questions; by answering his questions, you give him an opportunity to carefully listen, understand and respond to what you are sharing.

(continued on following page)

STEP 3:

Address your child's grammatical errors by modeling correct grammar.

Directly correcting grammatical errors can often backfire on you: your child may get discouraged or refuse to talk with you.

The best way to help your child is to restate what your child has said using correct grammar, modeling the correct grammatical form. This approach allows you to enter a non-threatening dialogue with your child while you model the correct form of grammar. Also, do not repeat your child's incorrect grammar as this will only confuse your child; only restate the correct form.

For more advice on modeling correct grammar, see page 69.

What To Do When Your Child Uses Incorrect Grammar While Speaking

WHAT TO DO:

The best way to help your child is to restate what he has said using correct grammar, modeling what's right. Doing this allows you to have a meaningful conversation with your child while you model the correct way to use language. When you do this, definitely do not repeat your child's incorrect grammar as this will only confuse you child; only restate the correct form.

Below are some examples of what to do and what not to do when modeling correct forms of grammar. Remember that it takes a lot of work to learn all of the rules around the English language, so constantly encourage your child to continue expressing his ideas with the language skills he has already acquired.

EXAMPLE 1:

WHAT TO DO:

Child: I **goed** to the movies yesterday.
You: You **went** to the movies yesterday?
Child: Yes, I **went** to the movies yesterday.
You: Cool. What movie did you see?
Child: I **see** "The Explorers."
You: You did? I **saw** "The Explorers" too! Did you like the movie?

WHAT NOT TO DO:

Child: I **goed** to the movies yesterday.
You (looking surprised): You **goed** to the movies yesterday?
Child: Yes.
You: I think you mean, "I **went** to the movies yesterday." Say that again.

(continued on following page)

EXAMPLE 2:

WHAT TO DO:

Child: I **is** tired.
You: You're tired? I **am** tired, too.

WHAT NOT TO DO:

Child: I **is** tired.
You (rolls eyes): Your grammar is incorrect. It isn't "I is tired," it's "I **am** tired."

EXAMPLE 3:

WHAT TO DO:

You: How many apples do you have?
Child: I have four **apple**.
You: You have four **apples**? I have two apples. How many apples do we have together?

WHAT NOT TO DO:

You: How many apples do you have?
Child: I have four **apple**.
You: No, no, no. When you have more than one apple, you say apple with an "S" at the end. You say it this way: "I have four **apples**. Don't make that mistake again."

Draw Me a Rhyme!, page 76

Phonemic Awareness
(Hearing, Identifying, and Manipulating the Individual Sounds that Make Up Language)

Mystery Toy

WHEN TO USE THIS ACTIVITY:

Use this guessing game to help your child begin to hear individual sounds in words. In the game, your child will listen to the isolated sounds of a word, and will then blend those sounds in order to figure out the word.

To become good readers, children need to distinguish the sounds that make up words. For example, your child should recognize that the word **cat** is made up of three sounds: /c/, /a/, and /t/. In "reading professional terms," this skill is called "phonemic awareness."

MATERIALS
- Box or grab bag with small toys in it (toy animals, cars, blocks, balls)

STEP 1:

Show your child the box or grab bag. Say: "This is my mystery box (bag). I have lots of different toys in here. [Open the bag or box and peak in without showing your child what's inside.] I see a special toy, and I want you to guess what it is! It's an animal. I'll give you another clue: I see a /c/ /a/ /t/ (say these three sounds of the word, not the names of the letters). Do you know what I see?"

STEP 2:

Allow your child to guess the word. If he doesn't guess correctly, say /c/ /a/ /t/ again and let him try again. If your child doesn't guess the object correctly, reveal the toy.

While holding the toy, ask your child to say the separate sounds and word with you: "/c/ /a/ /t/ makes 'cat.'"

STEP 3:

Using different toys, repeat Steps 1 and 2. When you think your child is ready, offer him your job so he can give you separate sounds to blend. Have fun!

OUT-AND-ABOUT **EXTENSION ACTIVITY** | Once you've played this game a few times, you can begin practicing these skills without the box of toys. For example, if you're out walking or driving you can tell your child that, "I'm thinking of something, and that something is a /c/ /a/ /t/ (say these three sounds, not the word). Do you know what I'm thinking of?" Give your child a chance to ask you questions.

Rhyme-Away Pictures

STEP 1:

Tell your child that you're going to play a game.

Say: "I'll start by drawing a picture. As I draw, your job is to carefully watch what I draw. Afterwards, I'll read a rhyme, but I will leave the last word out. Guess what the word is. After we figure out what it is, you'll erase that part of the picture."

STEP 2:

Draw or trace Rhyme-Away Picture Number 1 (page 74) onto a piece of paper with a pencil or onto a small dry erase board with a marker.

STEP 3:

Say each phrase on the page except the underlined word. Ask your child to guess the missing word. When she guesses the word correctly, cheer and ask her to erase the corresponding portion of the picture.

If your child does not identify the correct words, allow her to take a few guesses before giving her hints, and then eventually offer the correct word. When you give the correct word, say (for example): "Look at my mouth when I say these two words: 'said' and 'head.' These words rhyme because they sound like each other. Said and head sound alike. 'Said' and 'cat' don't rhyme."

STEP 4:

After you have read all your rhymes, your picture will vanish before you! Now have fun erasing Rhyme-Away Picture number 2 (page 75)!

Rhyme-Away Picture #1 Sheet

Directions: Draw the picture below. Read each phrase to your child except the rhyming <u>underlined</u> word. Ask your child to guess the missing word. Once your child guesses the correct word, she can erase the corresponding portion of the picture.

Illustration by Grace May Chiu

Go for a **run**,
then erase the <u>sun</u>.

If you know the **word**,
erase the <u>bird</u>.

Have you seen Ms. **Lindo**?
Erase one <u>window</u>.

Drink some **tea**,
then erase the <u>tree</u>.

You're such a **pro**!
Erase another <u>window</u>.

When you do your **chore**,
erase the <u>door</u>.

If you're listening to **me**,
erase the <u>chimney</u>.

Quick as a **mouse**,
erase the <u>house</u>!

You have the **power**,
erase the <u>flower</u>.

It might make **sense**
to erase the <u>fence</u>.

Let's not make a **sound**,
and erase the <u>ground</u>.

Rhyme-Away Picture #2 Sheet

Directions: Draw the picture below. Read each phrase to your child except the rhyming underlined word. Ask your child to guess the missing word. Once your child guesses the correct word, she can erase the corresponding portion of the picture.

If he **blows**,
erase his <u>nose</u>.

He won't know **why**
we erased one <u>eye</u>.

Go play in the **sand**!
Erase one <u>hand</u>.

Look up **high**.
Erase an <u>eye</u>.

If we **share**,
we can erase his <u>hair</u>.

I'll give three **cheers**
when you erase his <u>ears</u>.

Now let me **check**.
Yes, let's erase his <u>neck</u>.

He thinks you're **grand**!
Now erase his other <u>hand</u>.

After crossing the **street**,
let's erase his <u>feet</u>.

Let's clean up the **dirt**,
and erase his <u>shirt</u>.

If we don't see **ants**,
erase his <u>pants</u>.

He's on his way to **bed**.
Let's erase his <u>head</u>.

Illustration by Grace May Chiu

Draw Me a Rhyme!

STEP 1:

Tell your child that you're going to draw a picture together.

Say: "We're going to draw a picture together. I'm going to read a rhyme, but I will leave the last word out. After you figure out the rhyming word I left out, we'll draw it."

STEP 2:

Look at Picture 1 on page 77. Read each rhyme with the underlined word left out. When your child guesses the missing word correctly, ask your child to add a picture of that word to the drawing. Read all of the rhymes until your picture is complete. Note that there is no one right way for the end product to look so long as all of the object's parts are represented by whatever shape your child thinks best.

If your child has a tough time identifying some words, allow him to make a few guesses. If you need to, give him some hints and then finally, if need be, offer the correct word. When you give the correct word, say (for example): "Look at my mouth when I say these two words: 'said' and 'head.' These words rhyme. 'Said' and 'cat' don't rhyme."

STEP 3:

Now try drawing a second picture using the rhymes on page 78!

OUT-AND-ABOUT **EXTENSION ACTIVITY** When you're out to eat and are waiting for food, come up with your own rhymes for your child to draw. If other members of the family are around, some or all of you can take turns drawing or coming up with rhymes, making a fun piece of family art.

Draw Me a Rhyme! Picture 1

Directions: Tell your child that you're going to draw a picture of an alien together. Read each rhyme with the <u>underlined</u> word left out. Once your child guesses the missing word correctly, he can add parts to the drawing.

Let's go **ahead**
and draw a great big <u>head</u>.

Our alien likes to fly through the **skies.**
To see where he is, he needs two large <u>eyes</u>.

In order to smell a pretty **rose**,
our alien needs a long, pointy <u>nose</u>.

For aliens, happiness is always in **style**,
so let's give our alien a very wide <u>smile</u>.

To hold up its head, let's double **check**,
that our alien has a really strong <u>neck</u>.

Our alien needs food that is **yummy**,
so let's give it a nice sized <u>tummy</u>.

It loves to eat scrambled **eggs**,
but to walk to the kitchen, it will need
some <u>legs</u>.

If we want our friend to dance to a **beat**,
we'll have to give him a bunch of <u>feet</u>.

When I draw aliens, I never **fail**
to give my aliens a spiky <u>tail</u>.

What do you think of our outer space **thing**?
If we give it a song, do you think it will <u>sing</u>?

Illustration by Grace May Chiu

Draw Me a Rhyme! Picture 2

Directions: Tell your child that you're going to draw a picture of a clown together. Read each rhyme with the <u>underlined</u> word left out. Once your child guesses the missing word correctly, he can add parts to the drawing.

When drawing a clown, it is **said**,
it's good to start with a really big <u>head</u>.

You can't help but **stare**
at our clown's crazy head of <u>hair</u>.

Our clown loves laughter and **cheers**,
so why don't we give him two large <u>ears</u>?

Fired from a cannon, our silly clown **flies**!
We want him to see, so let's give him <u>eyes</u>.

Our clown should be able to smell, I **suppose**.
Let's give him a large and colorful <u>nose</u>.

Let's draw a line that is curved, show some **style**!
That line's not a frown, but a happy, glad <u>smile</u>.

Did you know our clown plays in two **bands**?
With all of that playing, he needs two <u>hands</u>.

Our talented friend likes to play the **flute**,
but he only plays it while wearing one <u>boot</u>.

And where's the other boot? Nobody **knows**.
Let's give our friend a foot with some <u>toes</u>.

Look at this! I think we're **done**!
Drawing clowns together is really <u>fun</u>.

Illustration by Grace May Chiu

Oops, I Broke A Word!

WHEN TO USE THIS ACTIVITY:
Use this activity to reinforce in your child's mind that individual sounds make up words. Your child needs this skill in order to become a strong reader.

STEP 1:

First, model the game for your child.

Say, "Let's play a word game together. I'm going to say a word, and I want you to break the word apart. I am going to say the word slowly, and then you're going to tell me each sound of the word in order. So if I say 'dog,' you should say '/d/ - /o/ - /g/' [say the sounds, not the letters.]. Let's try a few words together."

STEP 2:

Together, practice breaking words apart.

Practice breaking up the following words: ride, go, and man. These words will sound like this: /r/ - /i/ - /d/; /g/ - /o/; /m/ - /a/ - /n/. Help your child with each word, repeating the word after you "break" them.

Common Challenges Children Run In To With this Game:

- If your child restates the word without breaking it into sounds, encourage the separation of sounds by saying, "Yes, the word is 'cat.' Can you tell me all the sounds you hear in the word 'cat'? "

- If your child provides a partial segmentation of the word ("/c/ - /at/" instead of "/c/ - /a/ - /t/"), say, "Wow, that's really close. There are two sounds that still need breaking up: cat is /c/ - /a/ - /t/. Let's try another word that's like cat: hat."

- If your child responds by spelling the word ("c-a-t"), say, "Super! You spelled the word cat! That's very good, but what I am asking you to do is to tell me all of the sounds, not the letters in the word. Let's give it another try."

Words You Can Use with this Activity

bag b/ /a/ /g/
lay l/ /a/
keep k/ /ee/ /p/
race r/ /a/ /s/
fine f/ /i/ /n/
zoo z/ /oo/
no n/ /o/
three th/ /r/ /ee/
she sh/ /ee/
job j/ /o/ /b/
wave w/ /a/ /v/
in i/ /n/
grew g/ /r/ /oo/
ice i/ /s/
that th/ /a/ /t/
at a/ /t/
red r/ /e/ /d/
top t/ /o/ /p/
me m/ /e/
by /b/ /i/
sat /s/ /a/ /t/
do /d/ /oo/

OUT-AND-ABOUT EXTENSION ACTIVITY

While you're out driving or walking with your child and your child points to objects and asks, "What's that?" name that object for your child and then ask her to break it into sounds. You can also ask your child to name things you pass while driving and then have you break those objects into sounds. Once you break the words into sounds, you and your child can come up with a song or rhythm with those sounds. All of a sudden, you and your child will have your own unique song to share anytime.

Building Words & Stories Together, page 81

Beginning to Decode and Sound Out Words

Building Words & Stories Together

STEP 1:

Cut out the game pieces and spread at least two beginning pieces and two ending pieces on a table or the floor.

STEP 2:

With your child, match single letter "beginning of the word" game pieces (e.g., b, c, d) with the two-lettered "end of the word" game pieces (-an, -ap, -op). Only create real words.

Following are some examples of what to do. Rather than saying the letter names, say the sounds the letters or letter combinations make.

For example, you can say: "What word would we have if we put /m/ and /op/ together?" [mop] "What word would we have if we changed the /m/ in mop to /t/?" [top] "What word would we have if we changed the /t/ in top to /p/?" [pop]

STEP 3:

Make the game more exciting by telling a story to your child using the words the game pieces can make. When you get to where you'd say one of the words, stop to say the word's beginning sound and let your child find the ending among the game pieces. You may need to say the rest of the sentence to your child to provide important clues about the word you're looking for. You can also first say the entire story with all of the words and then say the story again with the missing words. Do whatever works best for your child.

> **Here's a sample story you can use for Step 3:**
> Sparky is my pet. He barks a lot, but he's a good **d**__. Sometimes, Sparky gets into trouble with all of his barking. Just the other day, a **m**__ came to our apartment to drop off a package and Sparky began barking so loudly. All of the barking scared the mailman. He got scared and **r**__ back into his **v**__.

OUT-AND-ABOUT EXTENSION ACTIVITY

As you and your child become familiar with building words and stories together, try telling each other stories with missing words while you're waiting for food at a restaurant or waiting in line at a store. Let your imagination run wild with your stories. Just be sure to provide your child with sufficient details so that he or she can make meaningful guesses.

Figuring Out New Words While Reading

STEP 1:

If your child comes across a word she doesn't know, but can read words similar to it, ask her to read the new word by relying on what she already knows.

So if the word your child has a hard time reading is **fish** but can read the word **dish** perfectly, point to **fish** and say: "I know you can read the word **dish**, so I think you can read this word. Doesn't it look like dish? Instead of the **d**, there's an **f**. Let's try to figure out this word."

STEP 2:

If the new word is a compound word (one word comprised of two words), remind your child that she may know part of the word already.

If the new word is **forever** and your child already knows the word **for**, cover **ever** with your finger or with a slip of paper and say: "You already know **for** in this word. [Now cover **for**.] Let's figure out this four-lettered word, **e - v - e - r**. We've seen **-er** at the end of a lot of other words: what sound does that make?"

STEP 3:

Extend your child's learning by making a "word pattern" list as it relates to the new word.

For example, you could say: "Now that you know **dish** and **fish**, I bet you know other words that end with **-ish**! Let's make a list. Since you already know how to read **fish** and **dish**, you can read **wish**, **swish**, and **finish**."

Scrambled Sentences
Ordering Words in a Sentence

WHEN TO USE THIS ACTIVITY:

Here's a quick and easy activity you can use before or after your child reads to you to help her with individual word awareness and recognition, as well as understanding of sentence order.

MATERIALS
- Two large index cards or wide strips of paper
- Scissors
- Pen or marker
- Plastic sandwich bag

STEP 1:

Print a sentence from a book that your child is familiar with on a large paper strip. Place this aside, this will be your master copy.

Next, prepare individual cards of each word from that sentence. For example, if your sentence was "I went to the store," you would create five separate cards with one word on each card (or just write the sentence out on paper in large print and cut out each word).

At first, start with only three or four word sentences or phrases like, "I can see." When your child has mastered this, add more words, up to six.

STEP 2:

Place the individual cards in a plastic sandwich bag. Have your child shake the bag and dump out its contents. Ask her to try to reconstruct the cut-up pieces to match the master copy in front of you.

STEP 3:

After your child has placed the cards in order, have her check her cards against the master card again. She can make corrections if necessary. Praise her when she recognizes that she needs to fix something.

> If your child is already spelling, have her choose a word from a sentence or phrase and spell it while pointing to the letters. You may even want to encourage her to try writing a sentence on her own.

(continued on following page)

STEP 4:

Read the sentence together again with your child, using her index finger to track under the words.

LEARN-AT-HOME EXTENSION ACTIVITY

Ask your child to come up with a sentence. Write it down on two pieces of paper. Cut up one copy (making individual words) and have your child reconstruct the sentence. This variation introduces the idea that each printed word represents a spoken word. Your child will also begin to see that printed words have spaces between them, unlike spoken words, which run together as people say them aloud.

OUT-AND-ABOUT EXTENSION ACTIVITY

When you're in the car, ask your child to point out or come up with sentences that you can use for this game when you're home.

Delicious Alphabet Soup, page 88

Beginning to Write

Mind Pictures
Developing Your Child's Abilities to Become a Clear, Persuasive Writer

STEP 1:

Start by telling your child one of your own stories, particularly something personal from your childhood. Be animated! Perhaps you'll share a story from one of your birthday parties, from a day at school, or from a family vacation.

STEP 2:

At the end of your story, ask what pictures your child saw in her mind as you told the story. Ask what she remembers most from your story. By doing this, you'll learn which details from your story worked best.

STEP 3:

Ask your child whether she would like a clearer picture of anything in the story. For example, if you shared a story about being chased by a bumble bee, your child might wonder, "How big was the bee?" "How did it feel to be stung by a bee?" "Did your face blow up?" "Did you cry?" Answer these questions by providing more details of your experience.

If your child doesn't ask questions, that's fine. Prompt her by asking excitedly, "And do you know how big the bee was? Do you want to know if I cried?"

(continued on following page)

STEP 4:

After sharing your story, ask your child to tell one of her own stories. If your child doesn't seem to have her story well thought out, ask the type of questions discussed in Step 3 to focus her and to lead her to be more specific. Complement your child for giving you a clear picture in your mind about what happened.

STEP 5:

While she draws her story, you can support her work by saying things like, "Oh, I remember that part of the story! That's where you…" Your child will have learned not only that she has stories to tell, but also that good storytelling means creating pictures or sounds or smells or feelings in people's minds. Even more, she'll have a wonderful story about your past to think about and cherish.

Delicious Alphabet Soup
Working on Letter Identification & Letter Writing

WHEN TO USE THIS ACTIVITY:

Use this activity to help your child learn to identify uppercase and lowercase letters, to help your child learn to write those letters, and to practice letters' sounds.

MATERIALS

- Individual laminated, plastic or foam letters you can buy or make with the Alphabet Stencils on page 143
- One large bowl
- One small bowl of water [Keep-it-clean alternative: Don't use water.]
- One ladle, large spoon or dipping spoon
- Paper and a pencil

STEP 1:

Fill half of the large bowl with water. You can add food coloring to the water to make it look like actual soup. Put all of your laminated alphabet letters in the bowl.

STEP 2:

Let your child use the dipping spoon to scoop as many letters as he wants into the small bowl.

STEP 4:

Ask your child to scoop out the letter from the small bowl that he wants to pretend to eat.

STEP 5:

Ask your child to recognize the letter and to say its name out loud.

STEP 6:

After recognizing the letter, ask him to write that letter on the piece of paper. You can use the Alphabet Letter Formation Motion prompts on pages 94 and 95 if you think they will help your child. Keep repeating steps three through six until your child has "eaten" all of the letters in the small bowl that he wants to.

LEARN-AT-HOME EXTENSION ACTIVITY

A bowl of alphabet soup makes a wonderful meal after this activity. You and your child can talk about what both of you thought about playing the game and can try to scoop out certain letters from your bowls at the same time.

Water-Painted Letters

WHEN TO USE THIS ACTIVITY:

Writing letters on paper takes fine-motor skills, skills that take practice to develop. Here's a fun indoors or outdoors activity you can do to help your child develop these skills while reinforcing how letters are formed. This activity is also ideal for children who need to "re-learn" the correct formation of specific letters.

MATERIALS

- Dry, outdoor surface or a table well-covered in paper or plastic that can protect the table from paint
- One cup, bowl, or bucket of water
- Paintbrushes
- Paint
- Keep-it-clean alternative: Markers or crayons and paper

STEP 1:

Give your child a small amount of water and a paintbrush.

STEP 2:

Ask your child to paint a letter by providing sound clues.

For example, you can slowly say: "Let's paint the last letter we hear in the word DOG. What sound is that? What letter makes the /g/ sound? Let's paint the letter you hear."

Encourage your child to paint LARGE letters so that she can really produce each part of the letter in detail. If your child needs to see the letter, definitely show it. You can use the Alphabet Letter and Picture Sheets on page 99 for this.

STEP 3:

If your child is having trouble, ask her to hold the brush. Place your hand over hers. With your hand guiding hers, paint the correct formation of the letter. While painting, describe the motion of the formation: if the letter is capital "M," you'd say, "Up, down, up, down." By doing this, your child can see, hear and feel the formation of the letter. To learn how you can describe other motions, see pages 94 and 95.

Writing Letters with Play-Doh®

STEP 1:

Show your child some of the different letters of the alphabet. Together, say the sounds those letters make.

STEP 2:

Ask your child to mold the Play-Doh® into the shapes of the letters you just reviewed. Both of you can also come up with words that start with each letter your child creates.

STEP 3:

Take turns with your child making any object with the Play-Doh® and asking each other what letter the name of the object starts with and the sound of the first letter of the object's name. (The objects you create can follow a specific theme, such as animals or sports. Maybe you create a make-believe museum!) If you want, both of you can then make the corresponding letters with the Play-Doh®.

PlayDoh®-Type Recipe

Materials: Make sure your child isn't allergic to any of the ingredients!

• Boiling water

• Salt

• KoolAid® or a similar substance

• Cream of tartar

• Flour

Recipe:

• Mix together 1 cup of boiling water, ½ cup of salt, and 1 package of flavored KoolAid® until dissolved.

• Mix together 2 tablespoons of cream of tartar with 1½ to 2 cups of flour.

• Mix dry ingredients gradually into the wet mixture using a metal spoon (KoolAid® stains other materials).

• When stirring becomes difficult, have fun and use your hands!

OUT-AND-ABOUT EXTENSION ACTIVITY

If you're at a park and are already in the sandbox, wet some sand with water and help your child mold letters out of the wet sand. You obviously don't want to turn this shared activity into what could feel like an assignment. If you tell your child to make letters and just watch her, it could feel that way. So definitely do the activity together and celebrate your child's achievements. Of course, the park is all about fun, so if your child would rather make castles or anything else with the sand, let your child's preferences win out.

The Glittering Alphabet
Learning to Draw and Recognize Each Letter

WHEN TO USE THIS ACTIVITY:
Use this activity to help your child learn to write and recognize each letter of the alphabet.

MATERIALS
- Glitter and glue
- Newspaper sheets
- Either 8.5 by 11 inch sheets of paper or similar sized pieces of construction paper
- A dark-colored marker

STEP 1:

Lay out the newspaper on the table so clean-up is easier! Then, with the marker, make large letters of the alphabet using dotted lines on the pieces of 8.5 by 11 inch paper (one letter per page). The Alphabet Letter and Picture Sheets on page 99 may help.

STEP 2:

Ask your child to connect the dotted lines with the glue.

STEP 3:

Let your child pour glitter all over the page and then ask him to shake it off onto the newspaper.

STEP 4:

Ask your child what letter has appeared on the page! Have your child say the sounds of that letter with you.

STEP 5:

Repeat with other letters of the alphabet. If you think your child is up for it, you can make both upper and lower case letters on the page, as well as short words.

Keep-it-Clean Alternative

Even with newspaper protecting your table or floor, a glitter and glue combination can get pretty messy. If you want to do this activity with your child while avoiding the mess try one of these alternatives.

Use Cheerios®. After you draw the dotted lines on the paper (see Step 2), have your child put Cheerios® or another type of healthy snack along the lines to create the letters.

Use Colored Markers or Crayons. Instead of using a black marker to make the dotted lines, use a light pencil. Then have your child trace over it with her favorite markers or crayons.

INSPIRATIONS & SOURCES

Some of the activities in this book were inspired by a number of tutors, teachers, authors and researchers outside of our organization, America Learns (www.americalearns.net). Following is a list of those inspirations and sources. We encourage you to check out the books referenced below as they're wonderful resources.

Alphabet Basketball (56) ....Douglas Christie, University of Michigan's America Reads Tutoring Corps

Alphabet Dice (50)...Myrtle Rowe, America Reads – Mississippi

Alphabet Letters and Sharks (45)................................. Amy Chajkowski, America Reads at the University of Pittsburgh

Alphabet Safari (46)...The City ABC Book by Zoran Milich (2002)
Published by Kids Can Press, Ltd.

Delicious Alphabet Soup (88)...Charlene Anderson, America Reads – Mississippi

Draw Me a Rhyme (76) .... Phonemic Awareness: Playing with sounds to strengthen beginning reading skills
by Jo Fitzpatrick (1997), Published by Creative Teaching Press. (p. 105-107)

I Can Read My Letters With My Eyes Shut! (49) .... Reading Games for Young Children by Jackie Silberg (2005)
Published by Gryphon House (p. 48)

I Spy a Rhyme (65).. The Between the Lions Book for Parents (p. 47)

Learning That Sounds in Words Can be Written with Letters (20)............................... Learning about Print in Preschool
by Dorothy S. Strickland & Judith A. Schnickedanz (2004)
Published by the International Reading Association (p. 57 - 58)

Learning to Write and Recognize Your Name (26) ....The Between the Lions Book for Parents
by Linda Rath & Louise Kennedy (2004)
Published by HarperCollins Publishers Inc. (p. 42)

Make Your Bed (51) .... Anila Bindal, University of Michigan's America Reads Tutoring Corps

Mind Pictures (86).............................. Craft Lessons: Teaching Writing K-8 by Ralph Fletcher & Joann Portalupi (1998)
Published by Stenhouse Publishers (p. 24)

My ABC Book (36) .... Marge Brege, University of Michigan's America Reads Tutoring Corps

Playing "Store" to Learn Letter Sounds (60) ....Reading Games for Young Children by Jackie Silberg (p. 17)

Quickly Reengaging Your Child in a Story You're Reading (9)...Jared Schwartz,
America Reads at the University of Pittsburgh

Rhyme-Away Pictures (73)............... Phonemic Awareness: Playing with sounds to strengthen beginning reading skills
(p. 102-104)

Things I Like (22).. Learning about Print in Preschool (p. 38-39)

Using Pictures to Work on Letter/Sound Identification (58) ....LaTanya Greenridge, University of Michigan's
America Reads Tutoring Corps

What's in the Box? (66) .... Linking Language: Simple Language and Literacy Activities
Throughout the Curriculum by Bob Rockwell, Debra Hoge, and Bill Searcy (1999)
Published by Gryphon House (p. 20)

Word Searching at Home (27) .... Learning about Print in Preschool (p. 40-41)

Zany Reading (29).. The Between the Lions Book for Parents (p. 44)

Materials

Alphabet Letter Formation Motions: Uppercase

For many young children, it helps to say these directional moves as they practice the strokes with you to form uppercase letters.

A   slant up, slant down, lift, across

B   down, around, and around

C   around and stop

D   down and around

E   down, lift, across, lift, across, lift, across

F   down, lift, across, lift, across

G   around, lift, and across

H   down, lift, down, lift, across

I   down

J   down and hook

K   down, slant in, slant out

L   down and across

M   up, slant down, slant up, down

N   down, lift, slant down, up

O   around and close

P   down, lift, and around

Q   around, close, lift, cross

R   down, lift, around, slant down

S   curve, slant, curve

T   across, lift, down

U   down, curve, and up

V   slant down, slant up

W   slant down, slant up, slant down, slant up

X   slant right, lift, slant across the other way

Y   slant right, lift, slant left and down

Z   across, slant, and across

Adapted from The Between the Lions Book for Parents
Linda Rath & Louise Kennedy (2004)
HarperCollins Publishers Inc. (p. 52)

Alphabet Letter Formation Motions: Lowercase

For many young children, it helps to say these directional moves as they practice the strokes with you to form lowercase letters.

a	around, up, and down
b	down, up, and around
c	around and stop
d	around, up high, and down
e	across, around, and stop
f	curve, down, lift, and cross
g	around, down low, and hook
h	down, hump
i	down, with a dot
j	down low, hook, and a dot
k	down, slant in, slant out
l	down
m	down, hump, hump
n	down, hump
o	around and close
p	down low, up, and around
q	around, down low, hook right
r	down, up, and over
s	curve, slant, and curve
t	down, lift, and cross
u	down, curve, up
v	slant down, slant up
w	slant down, slant up, slant down, slant up
x	slant right, lift, slant across the other way
y	slant right, lift, and slant down low
z	across, slant, and across

Adapted from The Between the Lions Book for Parents
Linda Rath & Louise Kennedy (2004)
HarperCollins Publishers Inc. (p. 52)

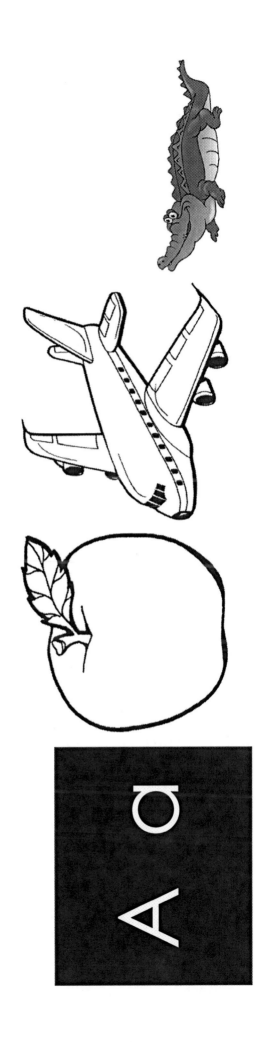

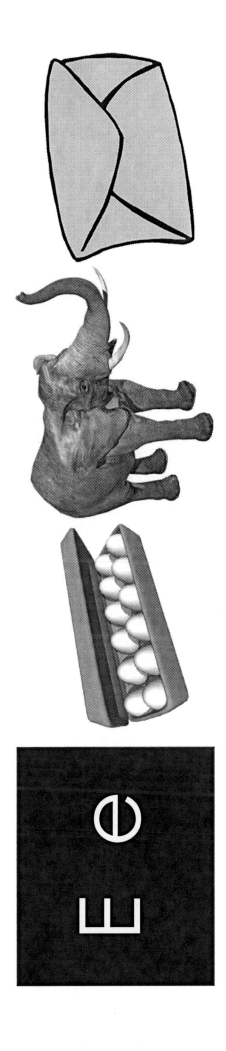
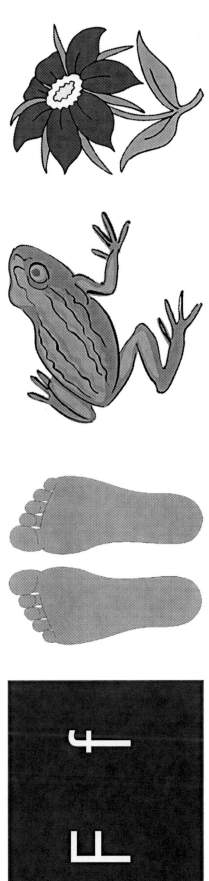

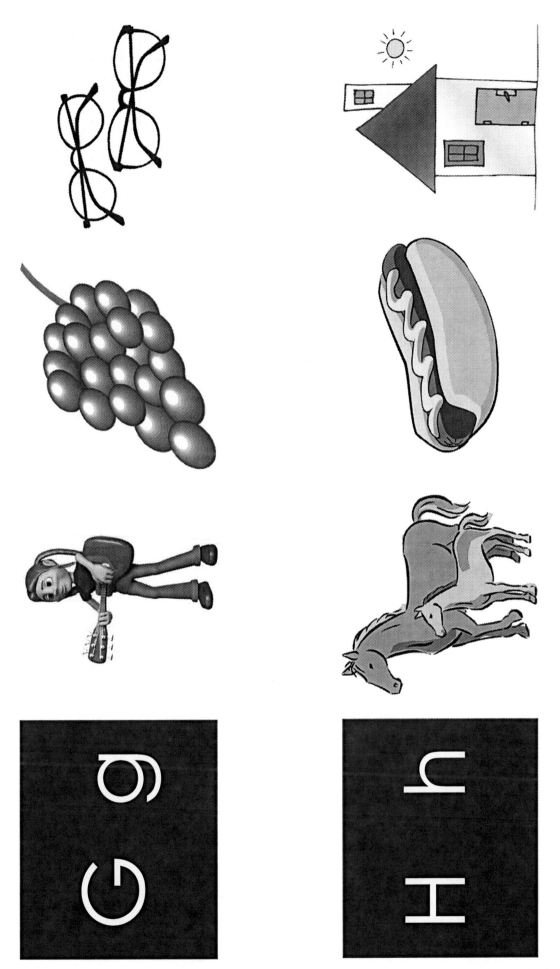

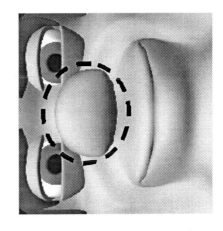

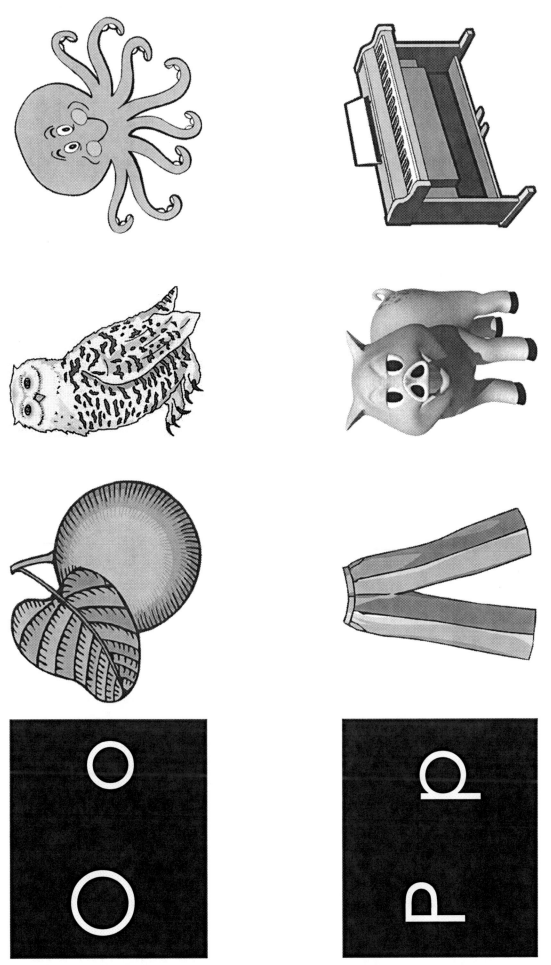

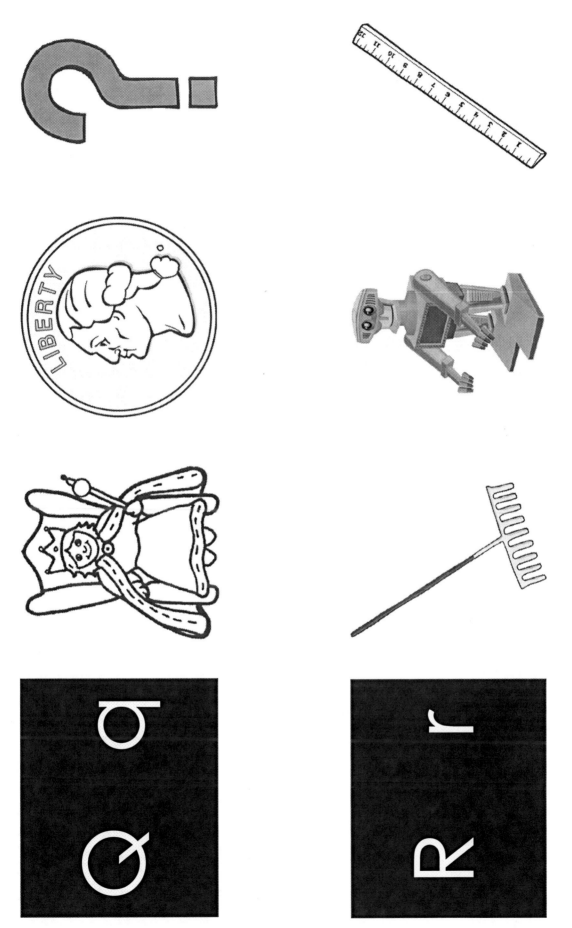

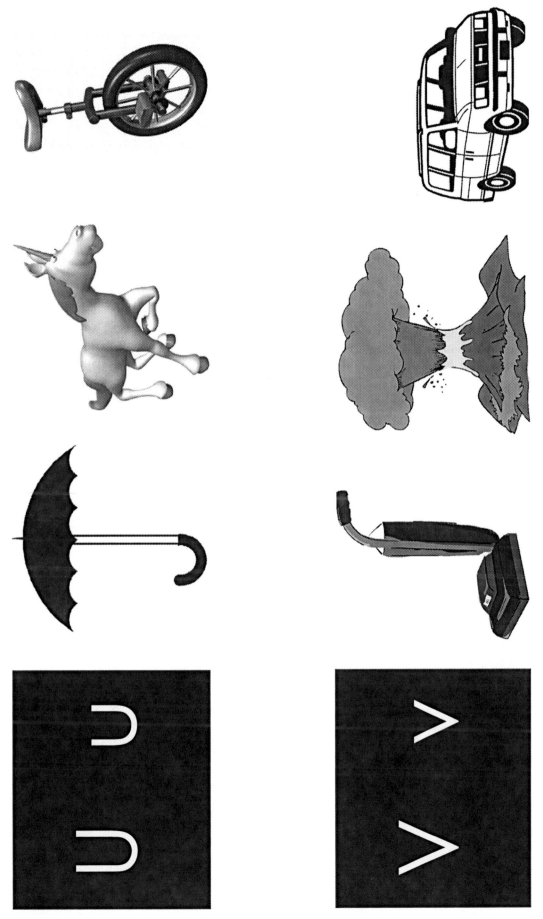

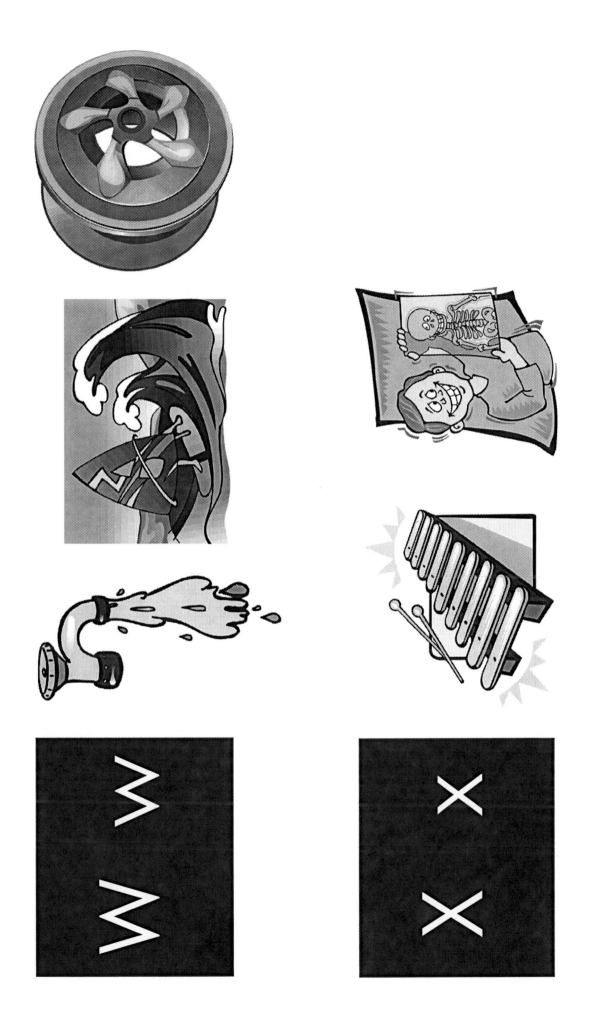

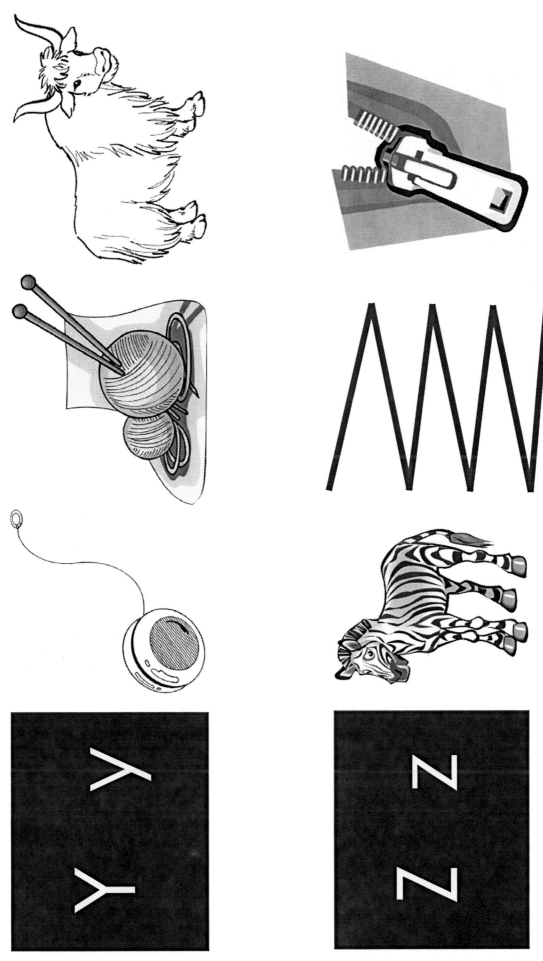

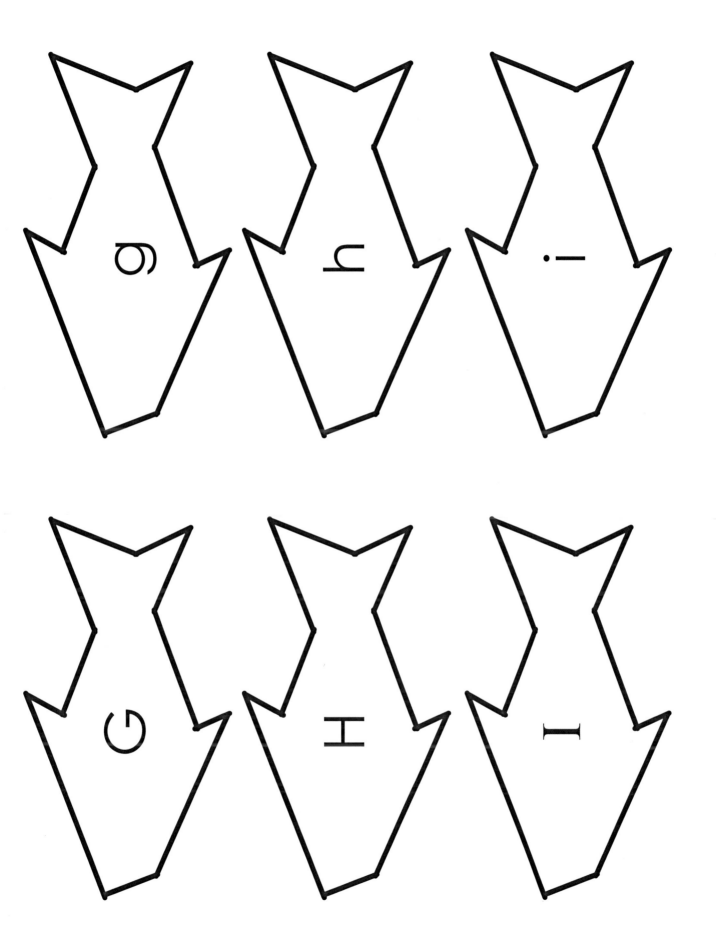

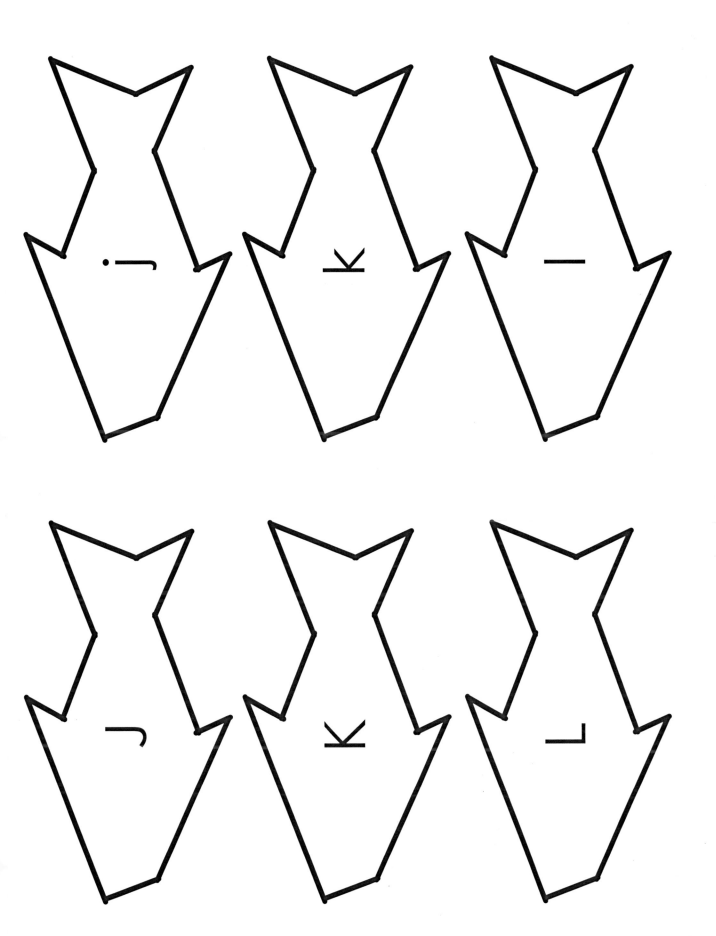

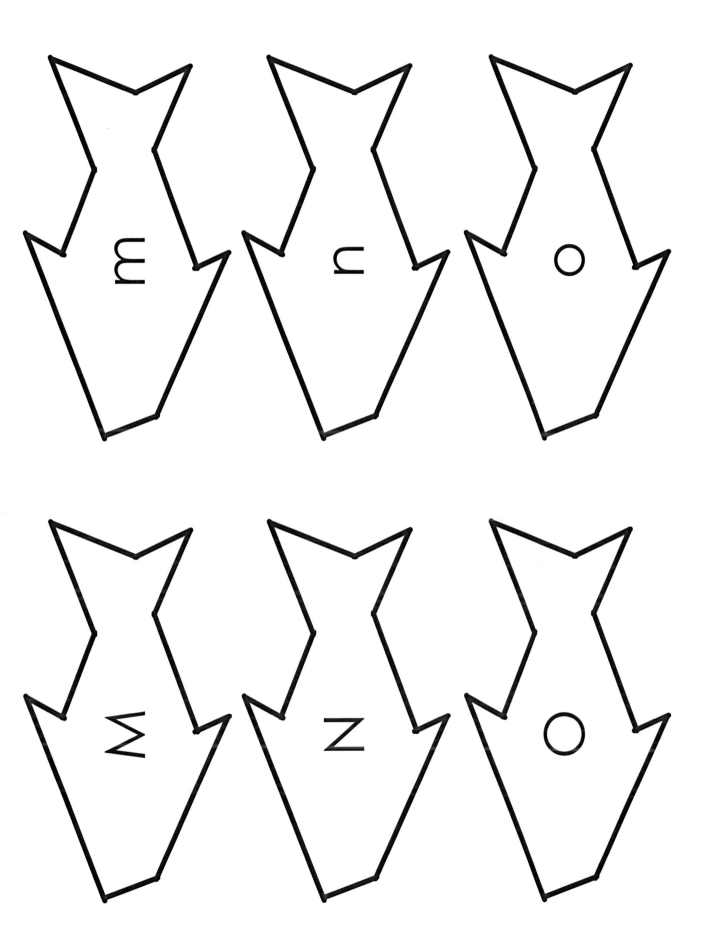

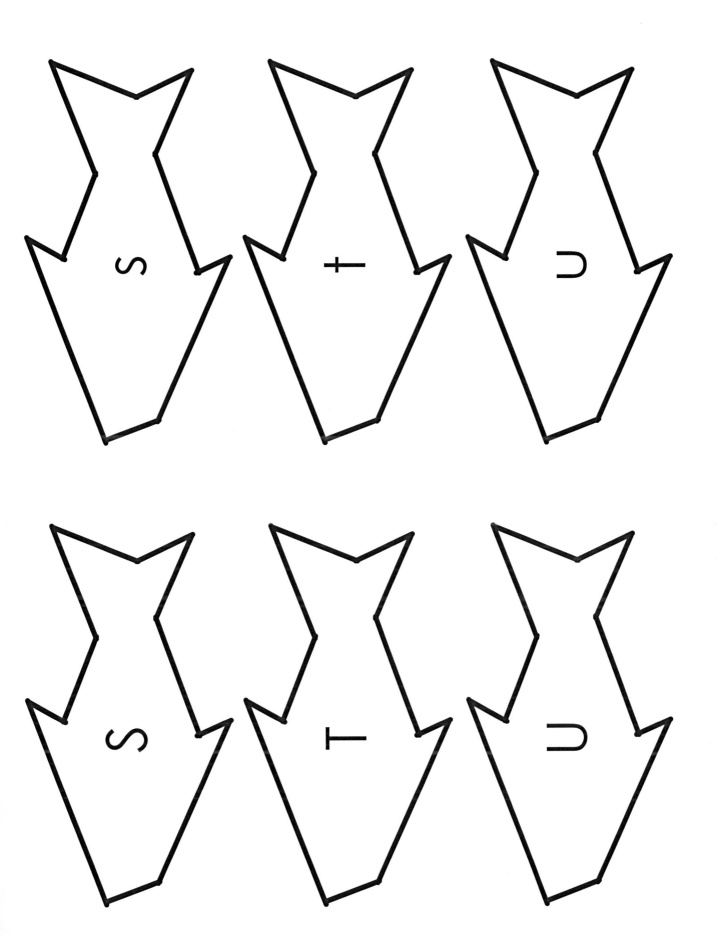

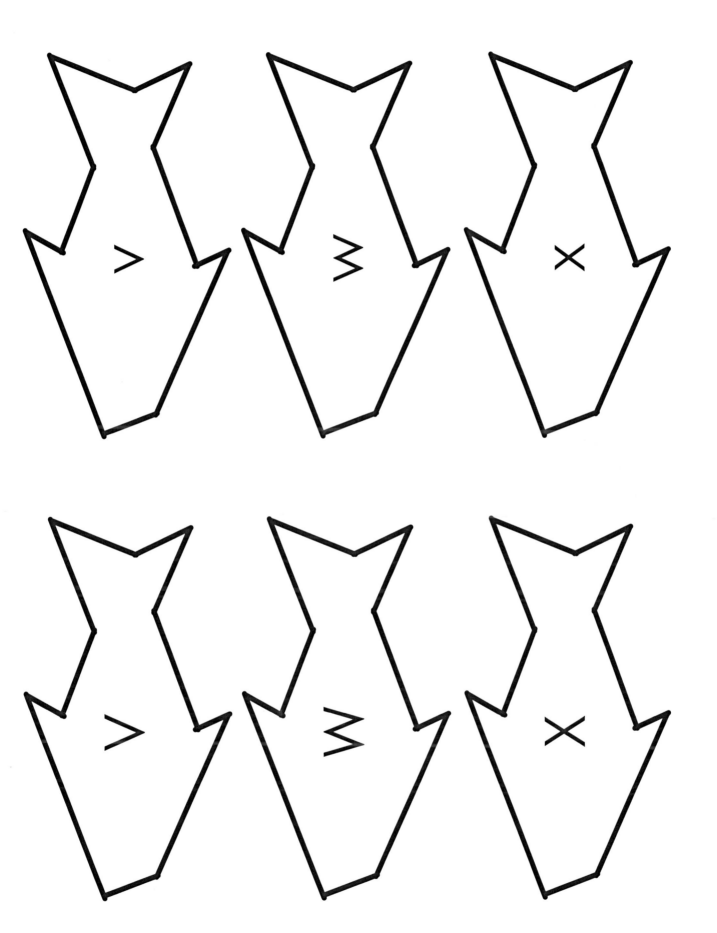

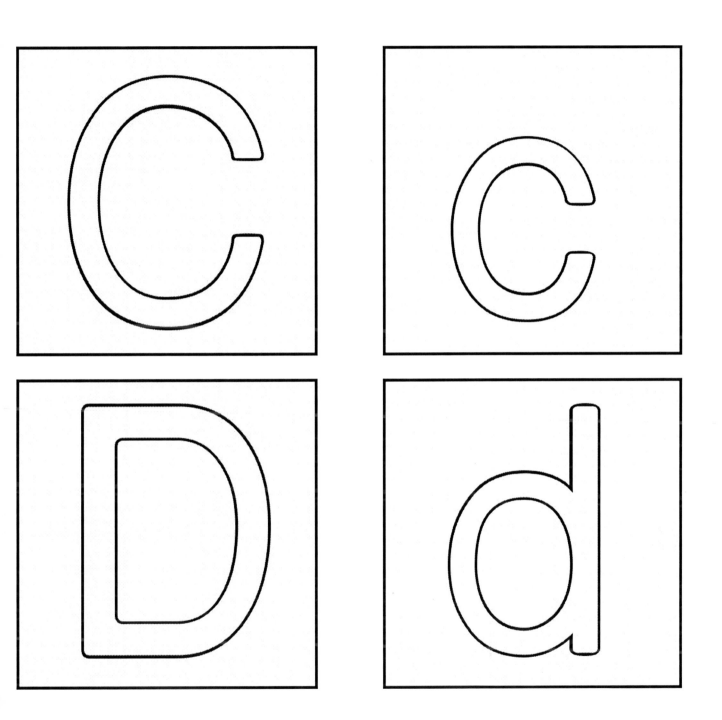

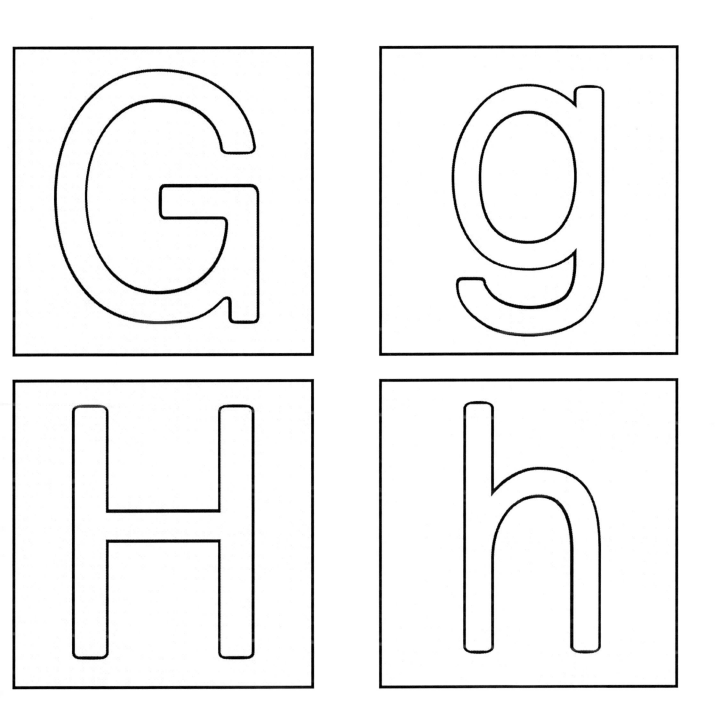

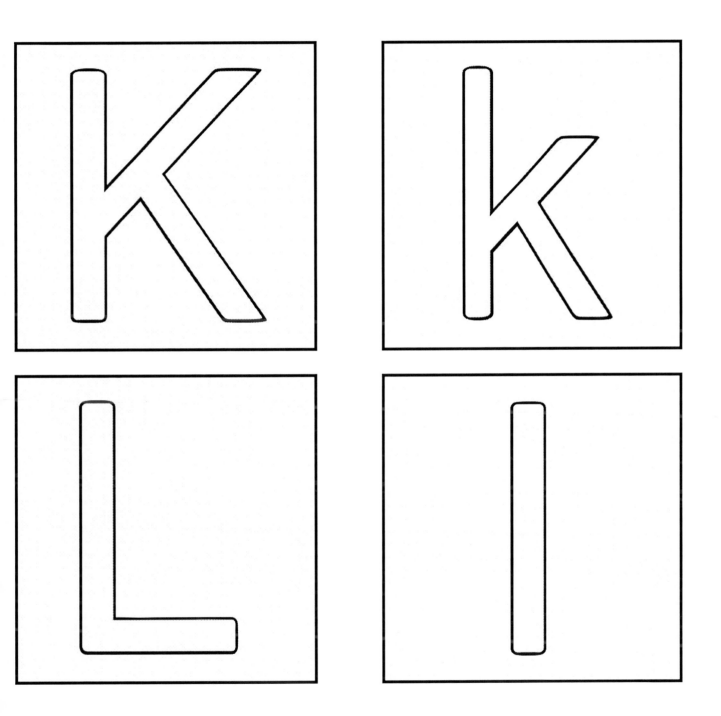

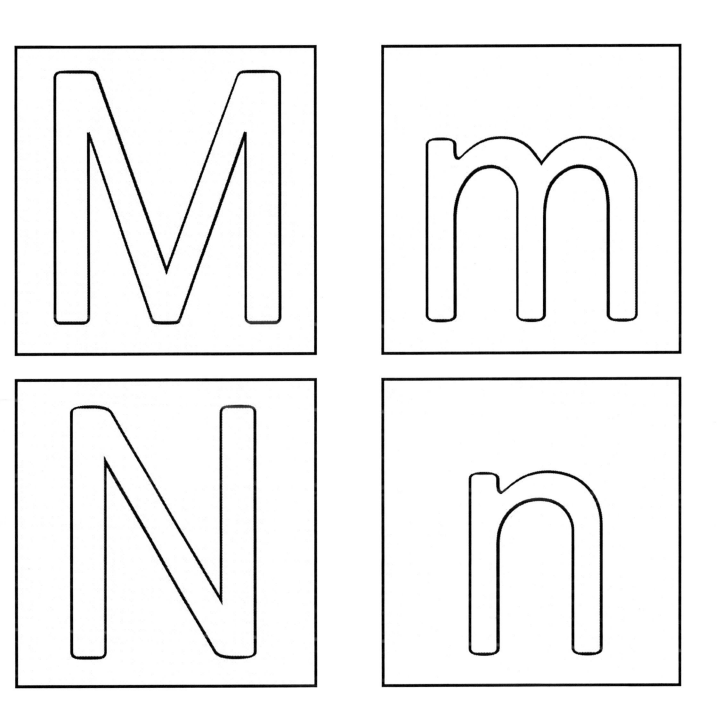

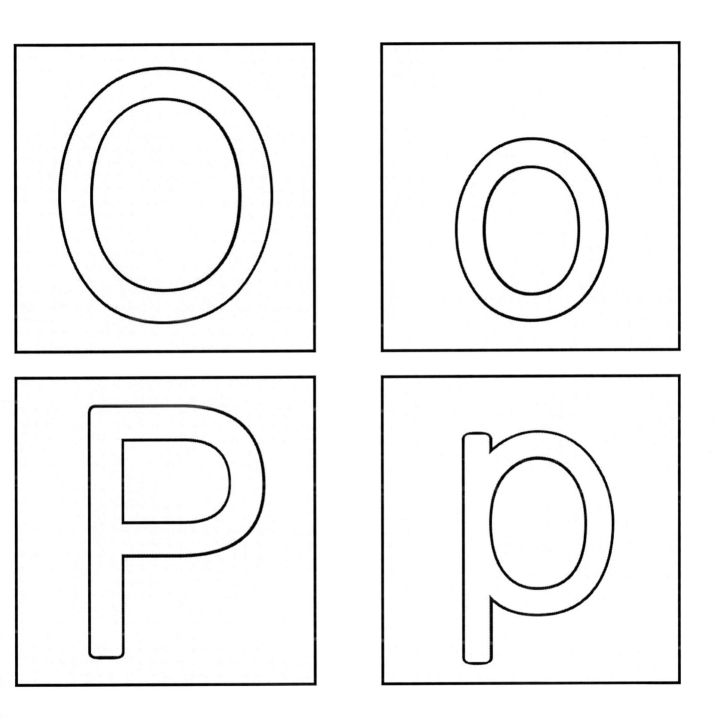

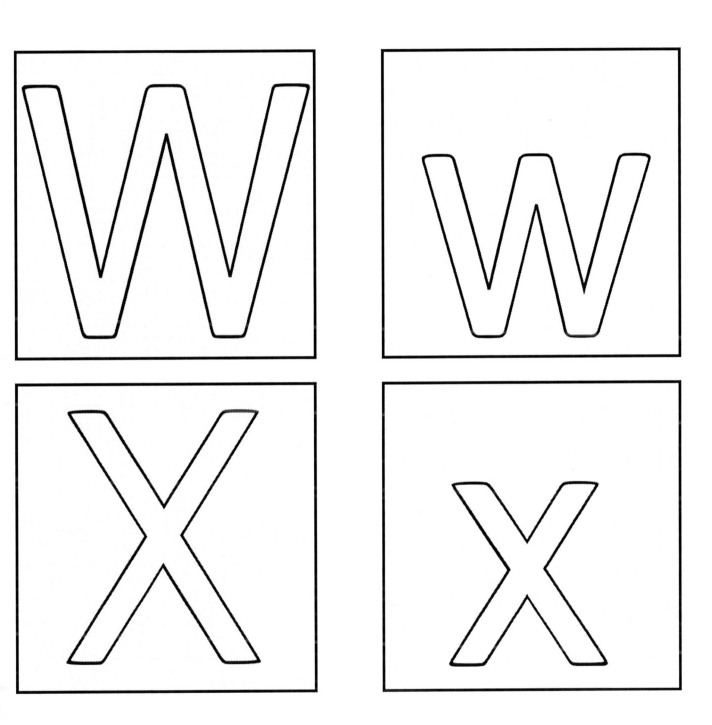

"Building Words & Stories Together" Game Pieces

DIRECTIONS:

Cut out the game pieces for your child. Help your child mix and match the beginnings and ends of words.

WORD BEGINNINGS (YOU CAN MAKE YOUR OWN AS WELL.)

b	c	d	f	g
h	j	k	l	m
n	p	r	s	t
v	w			

Game Pieces (cont.)

WORD ENDINGS (YOU CAN MAKE YOUR OWN AS WELL.)

an	ip	ap	it	at
op	aw	ot	ay	ug
in	og	in		

BOOKMARK TEMPLATES

Caring for My Books

I keep my books away from food and water.

I wash my hands before reading my books.

I turn the pages of my books very carefully.

After I finish reading my books, I put them away.

I always return my books to the library on time.

Printed in the United States
202741BV00021B/1/A